CONTROVERSY!

Same-Sex Marriage

Jon Sterngass

Marshall Cavendish
Benchmark
New York

Other Marshall Cavendish Offices:
Marshall Cavendish International (Asia) Private Limited, 1 New Industrial Road,
Singapore 536196 • Marshall Cavendish International (Thailand) Co Ltd. 253 Asoke, 12th Flr,
Sukhumvit 21 Road, Klongtoey Nua, Wattana, Bangkok 10110, Thailand •
Marshall Cavendish (Malaysia) Sdn Bhd, Times Subang, Lot 46, Subang Hi-Tech Industrial Park,
Batu Tiga, 40000 Shah Alam, Selangor Darul Ehsan, Malaysia

Marshall Cavendish is a trademark of Times Publishing Limited
All websites were available and accurate when this book was sent to press.

Library of Congress Cataloging-in-Publication Data
Sterngass, Jon. • Same-sex marriage / Jon Sterngass.
p. cm.—(Controversy!) • Includes bibliographical references and index.
Summary: "Allows readers to use critical thinking to create informed opinions on
where they stand on the issue of same sex marriage"—Provided by publisher.
ISBN 978-1-60870-490-3 (print) • ISBN 978-1-60870-642-6 (ebook)
1. Same-sex marriage—United States—Juvenile literature.
2. Same-sex marriage—Juvenile literature. I. Title.
HQ1034.U5S74 2012 • 306.84'8—dc22

Publisher: Michelle Bisson • Art Director: Anahid Hamparian
Series Designer: Alicia Mikles • Photo research by Lindsay Aveilhe

The photographs in this book are used by permission and through the courtesy of:
Cover photo by Kaadaa/Getty Images; Hill Street Studios/Getty Images: p. 4; Porter Gifford/Liaison/
Getty Images: p. 9; Wilbur Funches/AP Photo: p. 11; Manuel Balce Ceneta/AP Photo: p. 13;
Christopher Capozziello/Getty Images: p. 18; The Granger Collection, NYC: p. 28; Bettmann/
Corbis: p. 35; Ian Shaw/Alamy: p. 40; Carlos Sanchez/Stringer/Reuters/Corbis: p. 47; World
Religions Photo Library/The Bridgeman Art Library International: p. 51; The Fresno Bee, Christian
Parley/AP Photo: p. 53; David Friedman/Getty Images: p. 60; Britt Erlanson/Getty Images: p. 63;
Lihee Avidan/Getty Images: p. 70; Marilyn Humphries/Newscom: p. 78; k94/Zuma Press/Newscom:
p. 80; Bettmann/Corbis: p. 85; dbimages/Alamy: p. 90; David Paul Morris/Getty Images: p. 96;
Pat Wellenbach/AP Photo: p. 97; Alexandre Meneghini/AP Photo: p. 103; Newscom: p. 105.

Printed in Malaysia (T)
135642

Contents

Is gay marriage an abomination, a civil right, or a simple expression of love? At this wedding reception in California during a brief period when gay marriage was legal, it was a source of joy.

1 An Issue Takes Shape

ROMANTIC OR SEXUAL ATTRACTION AMONG PEOPLE of the same sex remains a divisive issue in the United States and around the world. A few nations decree the death penalty for those who engage in homosexual acts, while others guarantee lesbians and gay men the same civil rights as the rest of the population. Some individuals believe that homosexuality is an abomination; others see it as an acceptable expression of human affection.

Since homosexuality itself is a contentious issue, it is hardly surprising that same-sex marriage is far more controversial. Because marriage is an institution with both societal and religious dimensions—it involves the consent of the government, God, or both—the drive to redefine it to include same-sex spouses has given rise to strong reactions wherever the issue has been introduced. Religious authorities can choose to marry or not marry whomever they wish. The government's permission is needed, however, for a couple to enter into or dissolve a civil marriage, since in the United States civil marriage is the legal gateway to many benefits, protections, and responsibilities.

Several American courts have asserted that same-sex couples have a right to marry. "[T]he right to marry is not properly viewed simply as a benefit or privilege that a government may establish or abolish as it sees fit, but rather that the right constitutes *a basic civil or human right of all people*," ruled the California Supreme Court in the *In re Marriage Cases* (2008). As "a basic civil right," marriage cannot be withheld from same-sex couples, said the Court, and sexual orientation, like race and gender, is a protected class. Discrimination or classification that is based on sexual orientation must receieve strict scrutiny under the equal-protection clause of the California State Constitution. When the Iowa Supreme Court made a similar decision in *Varnum* v. *Brien*, it effectively legalized same-sex marriage in that state in 2009.

Decisions of this nature convinced some of its advocates that same-sex marriage was on an unstoppable path to approval, especially in the states of the U.S. Northeast. Legislatures in Maine, New Hampshire, Connecticut, and Vermont had all voted to legalize same-sex marriage. Similar bills in New York and New Jersey had political and popular support. "Every successful social movement eventually moves from the unthinkable to the impossible to the inevitable," noted Laura Listwood, founder of Women World Leaders.

Then a backlash set in. In December 2009, the bill to legalize same-sex marriage in New York failed by a margin whose width surprised its enthusiasts. In New Jersey in 2010, a similar bill was defeated by a vote of 20 to 14. In California, a decision was made not to try to reverse in 2010 the ban on gay marriage that state voters had approved in November 2008. Those opposing the ban realized they lacked the votes to overturn it. Voters in Maine repealed in 2009 a state law allowing same-sex marriage despite its supporters' advantage in money and volunteers. With the repeal, Maine became at least the fortieth state to reject same-sex marriage at the ballot box, by legislation, or by ballot initiative.

"Advocates for same-sex marriage have attempted to portray their cause as inevitable," said one same-sex marriage opponent. "However, it has become clear that Americans continue to understand marriage the way it has always been understood, and New York is not different in that regard. This is a victory for the basic building block of our society." How the issue will be resolved remains a subject of heated controversy.

Framing the Issue

The sheer number of homosexuals in the United States contributes to the contentiousness. In 2005, an estimated 8.8 million gay, lesbian, and bisexual people were living in the United States. According to the U.S. Census Bureau's tally, the country had at least 770,000 gay and lesbian couples (slightly more male than female) living together, and same-sex couples made up about one percent of all couples' households. About one out of every five same-sex couples were raising children under the age of eighteen. Also as of 2005, about 270,000 children lived in U.S. households headed by same-sex couples. This number includes an estimated 65,000 adopted children who were living with gay or lesbian parents.

The Gay Rights Movement

Although the Mattachine Society, one of the oldest homosexual-rights advocacy groups, fought as long ago as the 1950s to have lesbians and gays treated as citizens with rights equal to those held by "straight" Americans, the 1969 Stonewall Riot in New York City is commonly described as the beginning of the modern gay rights movement. By then, the 1960s revolution in sexual norms and conventions had led parts of American society to begin to reconsider their opinion of homosexuality. Changed attitudes were slow to reach the New York City police, who frequently raided the Stonewall Inn, a popular gay bar in Greenwich Village. On June 27, 1969, a crowd gathered on the street outside and watched the officers arrest the bartender and a few gay men. The crowd, which grew to an estimated two-thousand, was fed up with police persecution. Spontaneous acts of violence quickly became a riot. It has been described as perhaps the first time in American history that people in the gay community fought back against what they saw as government persecution. The Stonewall Riot became a symbol of resistance that inspired the gay community; within two years there were gay rights groups in every major American

States with Most Same-Sex Couples

California	92,000
New York	46,000
Texas	43,000
Florida	41,000
Illinois	23,000

Source: Adam Romero, et al., "Census Snapshot," Williams Institute, Decemeber 2007

Same-Sex Couple Households per 1,000 Households

- None present: 0
- Low: 0.01–2.99
- Med: 3–4.99
- High: 5+

8

The national Gay Rights March, organized in cities throughout the United States and in Washington, D.C., has become an annual event. But unlike the Easter Parade, it still elicits protests from those who don't believe gays have rights. Here, law enforcement officials separated antigay protestors from bisexual activists—the country has come a long way from the Stonewall Riot, the first time gay men and women protested against discrimination.

city, as well as in Canada, Australia, and western Europe.

In 1972, the National Coalition of Gay Organizations demanded several legal reforms, including marriage rights for all citizens. A court clerk in Boulder, Colorado, briefly issued marriage licenses to same-sex couples until the state's attorney general prevented further action. The marriage issue was not then a high priority of the gay rights movement. The focus was on ending police harassment, decriminalizing homosexuality, and passing nondiscrimination laws for the workplace and housing.

In 1972, *Baker* v. *Nelson* became one of the first legal challenges to the constitutionality of a state's ban on same-sex marriage. In this case, the Minnesota Supreme Court ruled that state law reasonably limited marriage to opposite-sex couples. The justices declared that the "institution of marriage as a union of a man and a woman, uniquely involving the procreation and rearing of children, is as old as the book of Genesis." The plaintiffs appealed, but the U.S. Supreme Court issued a one-sentence order dismissing the case "for want of a substantial federal question." That is, the Supreme Court did not believe that Minnesota's opposite-sex-only marriage laws violated the equal-protection clause of the Fourteenth Amendment to the U.S. Constitution, which says that "no state shall . . . deny to any person within its jurisdiction the equal protection of the laws."

For the next twenty years, courts in several states rejected the idea of same-sex marriage. In several states, including New Jersey (1982), Pennsylvania (1984), and New York (1990), courts heard cases involving property claims in same-sex relationships, but these cases did not involve the act of filing for marriage licenses.

The outbreak of AIDS (acquired immunodeficiency syndrome) in the early 1980s roused the American gay community to press the issue of civil rights for same-sex couples. Gay rights supporters were outraged when hospitals refused to allow same-sex lovers visitation rights and courts refused to acknowledge same-sex partners' claims in inheritance issues. The life-and-death aspects of AIDS raised a host of issues that led to the push for approval of same-sex marriage.

Advocates scored their first major victory in 1993, when three couples in Hawaii sued the state for illegal discrimination when they were denied marriage licenses. In the court case *Baehr* v. *Lewin*, the Hawaii Supreme Court ruled that the state had to show a compelling reason to restrict marriage rights to male-female couples. In 1996, after a battle of expert witnesses, the Hawaii trial court ruled that there was no compelling reason. This court's opinion was that the Hawaii legislature's prohibition of same-sex marriage was nothing more than discrimination based on sex. Same-sex marriage never became legal in Hawaii, however, because of the passage of an amendment to the state's constitution.

The outbreak of AIDS in the United States led to increases in both fear of, and hatred toward, the gay population as well as the beginning of acceptance. Here, two men comfort each other as almost 1,500 quilt panels bearing the names of New Yorkers who had died of AIDS were unfolded on the Central Park lawn on June 25, 1988, the first Gay Pride weekend.

The Full-Faith-and-Credit Clause

The Hawaii Supreme Court's decision in *Baehr* v. *Lewin* heartened gay rights supporters and discouraged opponents throughout the country. One reason for these responses was the so-called full-faith-and-credit clause, found in Article IV, Section 1, of the U.S. Constitution. The clause states, "Full faith and credit shall be given in each state to the public acts, records, and judicial proceedings of every other state. And the Congress may by general laws prescribe the manner in which such acts, records, and proceedings shall be proved, and the effect thereof." In effect, this clause requires states to accept legal actions of other states, such as marriages and divorces. The federal system depends to some extent on the full-faith-and-credit clause. Otherwise, the United States would be only a collection of individual states that could choose which laws of other states they would accept and which they would reject. People who were married or divorced in one state might not be considered married or divorced in another state.

The strategy of those pressing the case assumed that most state authorities would interpret the full-faith-and-credit clause to mean that if same-sex marriages were legalized in Hawaii, they would be entitled to legal recognition in the other states. Horrified opponents, who saw the tactic as a subterfuge to force the states to approve something the majority had rejected, reacted swiftly. In 1996, the U.S. Congress overwhelmingly passed the Defense of Marriage Act (DOMA). The final vote was 85–14 in the Senate and 342–67 in the House of Representatives. DOMA officially defined marriage in federal law as a legal union of one man and one woman. Under DOMA, the federal government does not recognize a same-sex marriage even if a state law recognizes it.

In 2004, gay residents of Massachusetts found themselves in a strange situation when that state allowed same-sex couples to marry: they were entitled to marriage benefits under state laws but denied them under federal law. For example, same-sex spouses

Representative Bob Barr (R-GA), left, was the author of the Defense of Marriage Act, which was signed into law by President Bill Clinton in 1996.

legally married in Massachusetts could file joint state income tax returns but not joint federal returns. If they moved to a state that did not recognize same-sex marriage, they were no longer married.

Residents of some states clearly felt more comfortable with same-sex marriage than those of other states. By 2011, more than forty individual states had passed so-called mini–DOMAs. Like the federal act, these legislative acts permitted states to refuse to recognize same-sex marriages performed in another state. At least thirty of those states wrote the federal definition of marriage into their state constitution. Same-sex-marriage advocates saw all these actions as attempts to circumvent the full-faith-and-credit clause.

Three Court Cases

Despite the passage of federal and state DOMAs, the issue of same-sex marriage refused to disappear. The earliest unsuccessful lawsuits in the 1970s, though brought in state courts, based their arguments on the U.S. Constitution. From the 1990s on, supporters tried a different tack. Because American marriage laws are state laws, more recent lawsuits have mostly been based on state constitutional arguments. Often, these arguments depended on sections in a state constitution that were not duplicated in the federal constitution.

This approach has proved much more successful. For example, Vermont's constitution has a "common-benefit clause," which reads that "government is, or ought to be, instituted for the common benefit, protection, and security of the people, nation, or community, and not for the particular emolument or advantage of any single person, family, or set of persons, who are a part only of that community. . . ." Gay couples in Vermont appealed to this clause in arguing that the state should not ban same-sex marriages. They claimed that marriage is a common benefit and thus could not be restricted to one type of individual or family.

In December 1999, Vermont's Supreme Court ruled in *Baker* v. *Vermont* that, according to the state constitution, same-sex couples were entitled "to obtain the same benefits and protections afforded by Vermont law to married opposite-sex couples." The court concluded that extending equal rights to gay and lesbian Vermonters "who seek nothing more, nor less, than legal protection and security for their avowed commitment to an intimate and lasting human relationship is simply when all is said and done, a recognition of our common humanity."

The court did not rule that Vermont had to grant marriage licenses to gay and lesbian couples. Instead, it suggested that the legislature could create a civil license that would give same-sex couples the same benefits they would have if they were married. After bitter debate, the Vermont legislature followed the court's suggestion and passed the nation's first civil union law. The *Los Angeles Times* wrote, "Supporters and opponents alike view it as the country's most comprehensive gay rights legislation—the boldest step in an expanding movement to extend legal benefits to gay and lesbian couples."

Vermont's civil union law went into effect in 2000; within three years more than five thousand couples had joined in civil unions in Vermont. The idea caught on in other states: New Jersey,

New Hampshire, and Connecticut all moved to offer civil unions as an alternative to same-sex marriage.

In 2003, two historic cases turned the debate over same-sex marriage on its head. In *Lawrence* v. *Texas*, the U.S. Supreme Court examined a Texas law that criminalized sexual conduct between people of the same sex. The Court concluded, in a 6–3 vote, that it violated the right of privacy guaranteed by the Constitution's Fourteenth Amendment. The decision reversed the Court's 1986 decision on the same subject in *Bowers* v. *Hardwick* and effectively struck down all state sodomy laws involving consenting adults. In short, the decision decriminalized homosexuality.

The justices in the majority in the *Lawrence* case specifically stated that they were not taking a stand on same-sex marriage. In the majority opinion, Justice Anthony Kennedy stated, "The present case . . . does not involve whether the government must give formal recognition to any relationship that homosexual persons seek to enter." In a concurring opinion, Justice Sandra Day O'Connor tried to limit the reach of the ruling: "Other reasons exist to promote the institution of marriage beyond mere moral disapproval of an excluded group."

The dissenting justices disagreed. They argued that the majority had "largely signed on to the so-called homosexual agenda" and that the end of discrimination against homosexuals would lead inevitably to the "judicial imposition of homosexual marriage."

The same year (2003), the Massachusetts Supreme Judicial Court (SJC) ruled in *Goodridge* v. *Department of Public Health* that the state may not "deny the protections, benefits, and obligations conferred by civil marriage to two individuals of the same sex who wish to marry." In a 4–3 ruling, the SJC noted, "The right to marry means little if it does not include the right to marry the person of one's choice, subject to appropriate government restrictions in the interests of public health, safety, and welfare." The majority decision described the right to marry as "a fundamental right that is protected against unwarranted State interference" and gave the Massachusetts legislature 180 days to change the law to correct the situation.

In 2004, the SJC ruled that civil unions, even if they had included all the rights and responsibilities of marriage, were not a sufficient remedy for the constitutional violation identified in *Goodridge*. For that reason, the SJC declared that lesbian and gay couples had a constitutionally protected right to marry. Over the next year, an estimated six thousand same-sex couples wed in Massachusetts. As of 2011, same-sex couples could still marry in Massachusetts.

In contrast, the highest courts in the states of Washington and New York found no constitutional guarantee concerning marriage or its benefits. Instead, in 2006, the justices in those states ruled that only the legislature could decide whether to permit same-sex couples to marry.

The Spotlight Shifts

In 2008, the California Supreme Court decided the *In re Marriage* cases along lines similar to those taken by the Massachusetts SJC in *Goodridge*. By a 4–3 margin, the California court ruled that limiting marriage to opposite-sex couples violated the state constitutional rights of same-sex couples. This decision in the nation's most populous state invalidated previously existing bans approved by the California legislature in 1977 and by popular vote in 2000 (Proposition 22). In June 2008, the court ordered the State Registrar of Vital Statistics and all county clerks to comply with the ruling and allow same-sex couples to marry.

Opponents of this decision drafted a ballot proposition, called Proposition 8, for the next election, which was only five months away. The ballot proposition took the form of an amendment to the state constitution: "Only marriage between a man and a woman is valid or recognized in California." In November 2008, after an extremely expensive (more than $80 million spent) and nasty campaign, California voters passed Proposition 8 with 52 percent of the vote. By restricting the definition of marriage to opposite-sex couples, Proposition 8 overturned the California Supreme Court's decision. A year later and three thousand miles distant, a similar situation unfolded. In May 2009, the Maine legislature approved same-sex marriage, and the controversial question was placed on the November ballot. Groups with names such as Stand for Marriage and Protect Maine Equality lined up on opposite sides of the issue. About half of Maine's eligible voters went to the polls; they voted by a 53 to 47 percent margin to reject same-sex marriage. As in California in 2009, and by a similar margin, gay couples lost the right to marry barely six months after they gained it.

In front of a cheering crowd, an opponent of same-sex marriage said, "Let's be clear. What the people of Maine had to say was that marriage matters, and it's between a man and a woman. This has never been about hating anyone, hating gays or anything. This has been about marriage, and only about marriage and preserving it."

These two elections led to the perception that only judges and politicians embraced same-sex marriage. As of 2011, voters in about forty states had banned same-sex marriage, and supporters had yet to win at the ballot box. However, advocates of same-sex marriage had a fallback position. One leading sponsor declared, "[O]ur rights as Americans do not depend on the approval of others. Our rights depend on us being Americans."

So the battle lines are clearly drawn, and there is very little room in the middle.

The voting results in Maine and California reveal an electorate almost equally divided between support for and opposition to same-sex marriage. Advocates believe that the initial backlash will fade and opposition will not be sustainable in the long run. Opponents dispute the idea that same-sex marriage is inevitable and believe the tide is turning. The one safe prediction to make seems to be that the issue of same-sex marriage will not fade from the American political arena anytime soon.

What is marriage, anyway? Does it have to be the union of a man and a woman? Is civil union an acceptable alternative, or is it flawed like the "separate but equal" laws?

2 A Brief History of Marriage

ONE OF THE RECURRING TOPICS OF THE SAME-SEX marriage debate is whether the concept of marriage between one man and one woman is eternal and unchanging. James Dobson, the leader of the Christian group Focus on the Family, claimed that same-sex marriage would lead to the destruction of "the family as it has been known for five millennia . . . presaging the fall of Western civilization itself."

However, others contend that what is now referred to as marriage has evolved throughout history and that it is almost impossible to give the term an authoritative definition. Marriage has been referred to as a legal contract, a natural or a civil right, a religious rite, and as a community-recognized relationship. In the United States, marriage implies a long-term intimate commitment to another person. Yet it is also a social statement, one that defines a person's relationship to and place in society.

In addition, marriage is widely held to have spiritual significance. In many religions marriage, because it is considered holy or a sacrament, takes place in a ceremonial context. The majority of Americans get married in a religious setting, although the percentage of those having only a civil ceremony is growing.

Definition plays a major role in the controversy over same-sex marriage. As one supporter put it, opponents often say that marriage is 'defined as between a man and a woman.' But marriage cannot solely be defined by who is excluded from it. It has to have some positive definition. Is marriage essentially a contractual agreement between two individuals to be defined as they see fit? Or does it symbolize and embody larger shared meanings that cannot easily be divorced from history, society, and nature?

The question of definition leads to even more questions. Must marriage be a permanent and exclusive union with no possibility of divorce? Are polygamy (having more than one wife at a time) and polyandry (having more than one husband at a time) acceptable forms of marriage? Can a valid marriage be intentionally childless?

One thing is sure: marriage is important in American society. In *Turner* v. *Safley* (1987), the U.S. Supreme Court ruled that marriage is such an important choice that it may not arbitrarily be denied by the government. The majority in the *Goodridge* case said, "Civil marriage is at once a deeply personal commitment to another human being and a highly public celebration of the ideals of mutuality, companionship, intimacy, fidelity, and family. . . . The decision whether and whom to marry is among life's momentous acts of self-definition."

Rights from Marriage

On some level, the American movement for acceptance of same-sex marriage is the fight of lesbians and gays to gain access to the wide array of benefits available to heterosexuals. One woman in a long-term lesbian relationship said, "If two complete strangers met each other last week and got legally married today, they would have more rights under the law than our relationship has after fifteen years of being together. That's not fair. We pay first-class taxes, but we're treated like second-class citizens."

Whether married couples should get special benefits is a separate topic for debate. However, it is undeniable that they do. Though federal law does not regulate state marriage law, it does assign rights and responsibilities to married couples that differ from those of unmarried couples. In 2003, the Government Accountability Office identified more than 1,100 federal laws or provisions in which marital status was a factor in determining who would receive benefits, rights, and privileges. In almost all cases, people's legal status improves with marriage. Unmarried same-sex couples face disadvantages in several areas, including the following:

- Death. Unmarried partners are not entitled to draw Social Security payments of the deceased partner or automatically inherit a shared home, assets, or personal items in the absence of a will.

- Health. Unmarried partners are not automatically considered next of kin for hospital visits or emergency medical decisions.

- Immigration. Unmarried partners from another country are not entitled to family unification or U.S. residency.

- Insurance. Unmarried partners cannot always sign up for joint health or auto insurance. Unmarried partners are not eligible for Medicare or Medicaid coverage.

- Legal privilege. Unmarried partners are not protected from having to testify against each other in judicial proceedings.

- Parenting. Unmarried partners do not have the automatic right to joint partnering, joint adoption, joint foster care, and visitation for nonbiological parents. Children of unmarried couples are not guaranteed child support and an automatic legal relationship to both parents. If one dies, the other (if not the biological parent) has no rights.

- Property. Unmarried partners do not qualify under real-estate laws that allow married couples to buy and own property jointly under favorable terms.

- Taxes. Unmarried partners cannot file joint tax returns and are excluded from tax benefits and financial claims specific to marriage.

On the other hand, opponents of same-sex marriage argue that gays do not face marriage discrimination. They make the argument that everyone is free to marry a member of the opposite sex or to remain single. They claim the government has a valid interest in promoting opposite-sex marriage because it leads to social stability and healthier child-rearing arrangements. Same-sex couples who live together can always make use of existing laws to protect their rights, such as by drawing up legal documents or signing over power of attorney.

Gay and Lesbian Opposition to Same-Sex Marriage

For many years homosexuals were a despised minority in American life. In those pre-Stonewall years, many gays and lesbians viewed their homosexuality as a declaration of rebellion against mainstream social institutions, including marriage. In particular, many feminist lesbians regarded marriage as an oppressive, male-dominated institution. In the 1970s, the Gay Liberation Front opined, "We expose the institution of marriage as one of the most insidious and basic sustainers of the system. The family is the microcosm of oppression."

Many gays and lesbians feared that same-sex marriage would mold gay life to conform to what they considered outdated heterosexual notions of love and monogamy. It might also split the gay world into "acceptable" married couples and second-class "outlaws" who would face increased discrimination. "Marriage is not the path to that liberation," said one opponent of same-sex marriage. The goal should be "providing true alternatives to marriage and of radically reordering society's view of the family."

For this reason, same-sex marriage was not a priority of the gay rights movement between 1969 and 1990. As late as 1994, a *Newsweek* poll of self-identified gay and lesbian respondents found that 91 percent thought equal rights in the workplace should be the main issue of concern for homosexuals, followed by 88 percent for equal housing rights and 77 percent for health and Social Security benefits for partners. Only 42 percent said that "legally sanctioned gay marriage" was very important, and 17 percent called it not important at all.

Even when same-sex marriage became a priority of the gay community, a vocal minority complained about the new approach. "We're frustrated by the suggestion that we should have to make our families look like straight ones in order to be considered a valid family by the government," wrote a lesbian couple. Another critic questioned, "If we are seeing marriage as a way to access health care, where does that leave people who are currently unemployed or who are single? We need to look at things marriage gives people and ask why that is conditional on being a couple."

Civil Unions

It has become apparent that the word *marriage* is politically charged and is a major obstacle to legalizing same-sex relationships. "Gay people should have all the legal rights that married people have," said one opponent, "but you can do that without bestowing marriage on them."

The result of this widespread attitude was the creation of civil unions and domestic partnerships. These legal terms created what might be called a nonmarriage marital status—one that involves some or all of the legal rights and responsibilities of marriage. This approach has been taken in the United Kingdom, Austria, Colombia, Denmark, Ecuador, Finland, France, Germany, New Zealand, Switzerland, and Uruguay, among other countries. Civil unions also exist in some states in the United States.

The main advantage of the civil union is that same-sex couples gain immediate access to the benefits of marriage. In a world without same-sex marriage, civil unions represent a big step forward for gay and lesbian couples in that they imply a toleration of homosexuality.

However, civil unions remain a compromise position. They were created to please people uncomfortable with same-sex marriage but unhappy with what they considered the inequity of the legal system toward gays and lesbians. Law professor David Chambers remarked, "Almost no one can be heard promoting domestic partnership. . . . Those who support traditional marriage say domestic partnership would undermine it. Those who support gay marriage say the state should settle for nothing less." Yet opposition from both ends of the ideological spectrum is not necessarily an argument against civil unions. An unsatisfying compromise is sometimes better than no agreement at all.

Same-sex-marriage advocates note two problems with the civil-union position. First, a civil union is not the same as a legal marriage. The California Supreme Court, in the *In re Marriage Cases* decision (2008), noted at least nine specific differences between the two in state law. It is still unclear what civil union means, especially regarding portability (the ability to carry the status from one legal jurisdiction to another). Almost all states and countries acknowledge a marriage, while domestic partnerships and civil unions have no universally recognized legal standing. Same-sex couples in civil unions cannot confidently carry the rights and responsibilities acknowledged in one jurisdiction across state or national borders.

Second, many gay men and women think civil unions were a good first step but an insufficient one. "Anything less than marriage really isn't enough," one gay man said. "If civil union has all the benefits—every single one—that marriage gives you, it's still a different word. It's a different psychological thing. As gay people, we're not the same. We're different. We're less."

Because civil unions do not include the word marriage, they seem to consign participants to second-class citizenship. Supporters of same-sex marriage often compare this status to the "separate but equal" status of African Americans under legislated segregation. "Some say let's choose another route and give gay folks some legal rights but call it something other than marriage," said one African-American supporter of same-sex marriage. "We have been down that road before in this country. Separate is not equal. The rights to liberty and happiness belong to each of us and on the same terms, without regard to either skin color or sexual orientation."

In *Brown* v. *Board of Education* (1954), the U.S. Supreme Court ruled that "separate but equal" was unconstitutional because the schools and facilities for blacks were inferior to those of whites. Using the same reasoning, the highest courts in Massachusetts, Connecticut, and California have ruled that their state constitutions did not permit same-sex couples to be deprived of full marriage rights.

A Brief History of Marriage in Europe

In marriage's earliest form, no governmental approval at all was necessary. Marriages were formed by families and recognized by the community, not the government. In agricultural societies before the Industrial Revolution, fathers and husbands-to-be arranged marriages on the basis of economic or political considerations with the main goal of providing legitimate offspring. Women had little or no say in the choice of their spouse. Love and marriage were unrelated categories in most cultures, and men did not usually look to their wives for companionship or sexual satisfaction. Marriage began as a property arrangement, and few pairings depended on emotional considerations. Inheritance was more important than feelings, and marriage was not a relationship between equal partners. For most of recorded history, the institution of marriage gave the husband customary and legal power over his wife. A wife was considered the property of her husband, whom she was expected to obey.

It is impossible to define clearly the meaning of "marriage" in ancient classical texts. The institution was important in Greek society, but the state did not legally recognize matrimony. Marriages were alliances of families and not certified or registered by the government. Ancient Greek law intervened in marriages only when questions of legitimacy, inheritance, and citizenship needed to be resolved.

In the Roman republic and empire, too, marriage was primarily a private arrangement concerned with property. The state regulated property and children and prohibited different social classes from marrying one another, but no government certification of marriage was necessary under Roman law. Roman males did not look to marriage to fulfill erotic needs and almost all kept concubines, or mistresses, maintained in a long-standing relationship for the man's sexual fulfillment. Some individuals from the start were able to make satisfying marriages based on emotional intimacy and personal feelings. Others came to love each other over time as they managed their household, raised their children, and shared life's experiences. However, the institution itself served primarily social and economic needs.

In the Middle Ages, from about 500 to 1500 CE, Christianity dominated European culture. In the first half of this period, the Catholic Church made very little effort to regulate marriage. In fact, the Church viewed celibacy as the spiritual ideal. Yet the Church permitted priests to marry and have children until the Gregorian reforms of the eleventh century. Not until the Fourth Lateran Council in 1215 did the Catholic Church officially declare marriage a sacrament that required ecclesiastical involvement. From the thirteenth to the sixteenth centuries, the Church's canon-law regulations concerning marriage were essentially the marriage law of Europe. A civil-law or common-law marriage, where it even existed, was usually supplemental in nature and carried less juridical weight. In 1563, the Catholic Council of Trent clarified the matter by declaring invalid any marriage not performed by a parish priest.

By then, the Protestant Reformation had introduced a radically different vision of marriage into the European tradition. Protestants believed marriage was a public and secular institution that the state had a right to regulate. They particularly wanted to break the Catholic Church's monopoly on marriage. In the Reformation, Protestants abandoned the idea that virginity, celibacy, and monasticism were superior to marriage and urged their own clergy to marry. By rejecting the sacramental character of marriage, Protestants introduced divorce in the modern sense—that is, with the right to remarry.

By the 1800s, the Protestant view dominated much of northern Europe. As early as 1753, the English parliament passed a law containing marriage regulations that involved licensing and the signing and dating of registries. Marriage in Europe had become a legal contract between a man and a wife overseen by the state.

Another dramatic change in modern societies was the elevation of romantic love as the motivating force in most marriages. The change began with the medieval troubadours who exalted courtly love and tied romance and fidelity to heterosexual intimacy. The Romantic movement in art and literature in the late 1700s and early 1800s helped spread the idea that emotional life should trump rationality. The secularization of marriage and divorce resulted in greater individual freedom. Industrialization raised the economic status of women and gave them more occupational choices. With increasing mobility and urbanization, parents began to lose influence over the marital choices of their children.

By the second half of the twentieth century, romantic love had

The view of marriage changed during the Protestant Reformation. Not only was celibacy no longer considered superior to marriage, but the clergy were encouraged to marry. Here, Martin Luther, the leader of the Reformation, weds former nun Katharina von Bora, in 1525.

become the most important factor in choosing a marriage partner. People chose to remain single rather than enter a loveless marriage; others who had married sought divorce when they fell out of love. The expectation of long-lasting romance led to an unprecedented weakening of the institution of marriage.

The Transformation of Modern American Marriage

European models of marriage traveled across the Atlantic Ocean to America during its colonization by Europeans in the 1600s and 1700s. Americans accepted most of the Christian norms of sex and marriage, including the understanding that marriage was a heterosexual and monogamous union. Like European Protestants, American Protestants permitted ministers to marry, tolerated religious intermarriage (at least with members of other Protestant denominations), and allowed divorce on proof of fault. Utopian communities attempted to create new forms of marriage in the 1800s. Among them were the Shakers, who advocated celibacy; the Mormons, who practiced polygamy; and the Oneida Community of upstate New York, who promoted group marriage. All these attempts were either failures or extremely unpopular with the wider society.

One distinct difference was the prevalence of common-law marriages in early American society. A common-law marriage exists when the community accepts as valid a marriage not formally registered with the state. Many Americans lived in sparsely populated areas where no governmental official was available to perform a wedding. Couples who made common-law marriages might be legally recognized as married only long afterward. However, the urbanization and industrialization of the United States in the late 1800s led to a marriage-reform movement. Witnesses, formal ceremonies, licensing, and registration had become common aspects of American marriages by the early 1900s.

After several centuries of American history, the institution of marriage has changed considerably. For example, wives have won more rights, and in 1967, the Supreme Court overturned state bans on interracial marriages. The steady liberalization of divorce laws, which its advocates linked to individual freedom and choice, was a very significant change.

Since the 1960s, American marriage has been in a state of flux. Beginning with the sexual revolution of that decade, many Americans delayed marriage into their thirties and beyond, divorce rates rose steeply, and remarriage and blended families (in which one or both members of the couple have children from a previous relationship) became common. Although Americans theoretically hold marriage in high esteem, in 2011 almost half of all marriages ended in divorce, and marriage rates were declining to record lows. At the same time, the number of unmarried couples living together exceeded 10 million (8 percent of U.S. coupled households). About one-quarter of American children are born out of wedlock, and the United States has the lowest percentage (63 percent) among Western nations of children who grow up with both biological parents. Many Americans look upon these statistics with concern, and the controversy over same-sex marriage must be viewed against this background. While supporters see it as an issue of legal equality and fairness, opponents contend that same-sex marriage will only hasten the decline of the institution of marriage in America and Europe.

Homosexuality in Western History

The term *homosexual* was first used in the 1800s to describe a person with a sexual and emotional interest in members of his or her own sex. Were there homosexuals before the 1800s? The issue is politically charged and hotly disputed. Clearly there were people who engaged in homosexual acts, but saying they had a homosexual identity may be introducing a modern view of sexuality that was alien to the times. Most people who lived before the Industrial Revolution viewed sexual acts as homosexual or heterosexual, but they generally did not assign a label to the people performing the acts.

Still, homosexual feelings and behaviors have been quite common in nearly all cultures. In classical Greece, the ideal union among the elite was male homosexual, and the Greeks considered same-sex attraction natural and common. The city-states of Athens, Sparta, and Thebes celebrated love between males as a guarantee of military efficiency, courage in battle, and civic freedom. It was a source of inspiration in art and poetry, applauded in theaters and assemblies, and praised by philosophers such as Plato. Sappho, a female poet, wrote about passion and love involving both genders. The word *lesbian* derives from Lesbos, the

Adelphopoiesis— the Creation of a Brother

In 1994, John Boswell, a Harvard historian, created a firestorm when he argued that "same-sex unions" had been an accepted part of the Christian church in the Middle Ages. As evidence, he presented Greek documents for a church ritual called *adelphopoiesis*, "creation of a brother." Using various symbols, the ceremony made two men brothers in the confines of the church. All of the *adelphopoiesis* documents relate to Greece, the Balkans, and the eastern Mediterranean between about 1100 and 1600, although they probably reflect practices that date back to the end of the Western Roman Empire in the fifth century.

Was the *adelphopoiesis* ceremony a same-sex marriage? That would depend largely on the definition of marriage. It was certainly not meant as a replacement for or threat to heterosexual marriage. It probably did not precede the formation of a common household or a family unit. Yet Boswell, a Catholic, believed it was "unequivocally a marriage" if one believed marriage to be "a permanent emotional union acknowledged in some way by the community."

Boswell's thesis has probably generated more heat than light. His interpretation of the ceremony was contested by the Greek Orthodox Church, which sees the *adelphopoiesis* ceremony as a rite of familial adoption. Other historians have criticized Boswell's methodology, translations, interpretations,

31

and conclusions. Yet it is still difficult to state precisely what these ritualized relationships were or how erotic they became. They may simply have been ritualized kinship rites with an emphasis on safety and trust. In other cases, though, they may have served as cover for a same-sex relationship.

The medieval French *affrèrement* ceremony may have served similar purposes. It was a common contract that provided the foundation for nonnuclear households and shared many characteristics of marriage contracts. While not its primary purpose, the *affrèrement* offered a way for two single, unrelated men to express their love and arrange to live with each other.

The French essayist Montaigne may have witnessed an *adelphopoiesis*-like ceremony performed in 1578. He later wrote in his journal that he heard that in Rome, "they married one another, male to male, at Mass, with the same ceremonies with which we perform our marriages, read the same marriage gospel service, and then went to bed and lived together." The story does not have a happy conclusion; the Roman authorities executed many of those who participated by burning them at the stake.

island of her birth, while her name is the origin of the adjective *sapphic* (meaning "relating to lesbianism").

In ancient Roman society, people regarded homosexual interest and practice as an ordinary part of the range of human experience. In some forms, however, homosexuality was criticized. The Romans thought the acceptance of the passive role by men was worthy of contempt. They perceived homosexual relations mainly as a form of dominance and linked sexual passivity with the political impotence of boys, slaves, and women. Roman males viewed women as existing to serve men in sexual intercourse. To them, sex meant penetration and women cannot do that naturally with one another. When a man penetrated another man in anal intercourse, he used a male in the function of a female and blurred the line between maleness and femaleness. Romans divided people into those who did sex (adult male citizens) and those to whom sex was done (women, boys, and slaves).

Christian Europe, from the fourth century onward, regarded same-sex relations as *peccatum non nominandum inter Christianos*—the sin not to be mentioned by Christians. The Catholic Church condemned male-male sex as diabolical and immoral. In the early fifth century, Saint John Chrysostom in the Eastern Roman Empire and Saint Augustine in the Western were outspoken opponents of homosexuality. Yet although condemnations of homosexuality were commonplace in the early Middle Ages, the church displayed less concern with it than with other sins. Before 1000 CE, the church lacked either the will or the institutional apparatus to persecute homosexuals in a systematic way.

Beginning around 1100, however, a revulsion toward male homosexuality appeared in European popular, religious, and legal writings. This attitude was part of a general increase in European prejudice against anything seen as a supposed danger to society. Homosexuals, along with Jews, heretics, lepers, and witches, became objects of usually invidious attention. The charge of sodomy became an accepted weapon in the competition for political and social influence. Accusations of sodomy, among many other reasons, helped bring down King Edward II in England and led to the suppression of the Knights Templar (a famous Christian military order) in France. In France, Spain, and many Italian cities, legal codes after 1250 made homosexual activity punishable by death, usually preceded by torture. By 1300, sodomy had become a capital offense almost everywhere.

Dominicans and Franciscans, members of prominent Christian religious orders founded in the High Middle Ages, preached that sodomy undermined morals and character, led to natural catastrophes as a punitive consequence, would lead to collective suicide, and brought eternal damnation. Anonimo of Genoa (c. 1300), a judicial scholar, stated that sodomy was worse than murder. "Sodomy is so filthy and grave that anyone who commits it deserves death by fire." This type of invective led to more men and women executed for homosexuality between 1400 and 1700 than in the entire period from 500 to 1400. Catholics and Protestants competed in enforcing harsh laws, and the Inquisition in Spain burned sodomites alongside religious heretics. From the late Middle Ages until very recently, homosexuality has been one of the primary moral taboos in Western culture—"the sin that cannot be named."

From the time of the Enlightenment in the 1700s, European legal codes began to eliminate punishment for same-sex acts. Homosexuals remained pariahs, but judges became less prone to use torture or impose the death penalty. New laws hesitated to impose draconian punishments on what are now called victimless crimes. The French revolutionary National Assembly decriminalized sodomy in 1791; the Napoleonic Code of 1810 retained the change and spread it across Europe. Sodomy, once a capital offense, ceased being a crime at all in many places in Europe.

England, Germany, and the United States were among the last to change; all three nations retained their laws against sodomy until late in the twentieth century. In England, executions reached a peak in the early 1800s, and the death penalty survived until 1861. In Germany, homophobia was a basic part of Nazi genocide, and more than 50,000 homosexuals were convicted under Adolf Hitler's regime, and as many as 15,000 may have died in the concentration camps.

In the United States, most states abandoned the death penalty for sodomy in the early 1800s. However, homosexuals remained a despised group for at least the next century. Things did not begin to change until the publication of the Kinsey Report in 1948, which publicized sexual subjects that had previously been taboo.

The Kinsey Report revolutionized the way sexuality was thought of in the United States.

The sexual revolution of the 1960s led to a rethinking of American attitudes toward homosexuality. In 1961, the American Bar Association suggested that the government drop all laws regulating private relations between consenting adults.

The modern gay rights movement in the United States began in 1969, when the police raid on the Stonewall Inn, a gay bar in New York City, led to a riot. A number of groups immediately formed for the purpose of repealing of laws prohibiting consensual sex, as well as for legislation barring discrimination against gays in housing and employment, and for greater social acceptance of homosexuals in America. In 1973, the American Psychiatric Association declassified homosexuality as a mental disorder and declared it a normal variation of human sexual orientation. Most states outside the South eliminated their sodomy laws in the 1970s. Only sixteen states still had antisodomy laws on the books in 2003, when the U.S. Supreme Court in *Lawrence* v. *Texas* decriminalized consensual homosexual sex in the United States.

Arguing from History

Arguing based on the past is a tricky business. Just because something has been done in a certain way—for ten years or ten thousand years—does not make it the right way or the best way to do it. Even if the "old ways" were appropriate a thousand years ago, they might no longer be so. Many societies abandoned traditional views of slavery, of a woman's rights, and of the nature of other races because a majority of people changed their mind and decided that old ideas were false or wrong. Same-sex-marriage supporters take a similar line. They contend that in the twenty-first century, everyone should be able to marry the person whom they love and to whom they wish to commit their lives.

However, the traditional argument—that societies should not lightly change long-standing core practices—also has considerable power. Historically, marriage has been the union of a man

Some Cross-
Cultural
Comparisons

Most cultures, past and present, have not assigned to homosexual practices any special moral or psychological significance. Societies without a strong Christian or Islamic base often viewed same-sex relations with a tolerant eye and did not think of them in terms of morality.

In China, the philosophical and religious systems of Confucianism and Taoism frowned on homosexuality but did not consider it a sin. China lacked Europe's distaste for male effeminacy. As a result, China was more tolerant of homosexuality than late-ancient and medieval Europe. For centuries, same-sex relations in China were celebrated in art and poetry.

Japanese Buddhism also did not specifically express hostility to homosexuality. In Japan, the samurai code produced a philosophy very similar to that of the classical Greek city-states. It was traditional for a young samurai to apprentice to an older and more experienced man and serve as his lover for many years. The warrior class held the practice in high esteem. In fact, at certain times in Japanese history, love between men was viewed as the purest form of love.

Many cultures other than European ones have recognized and institutionalized same-sex unions. In seventeenth-century China (especially Fukien) and nineteenth-century Dahomey (West Africa), the institution seems to have been on a par with opposite-sex marriage. In many Native American tribes (before they were militarily defeated by American armies), gender roles were flexible—the "two spirit" tradition—and marriage between men was commonplace. How similar it was to contemporary lesbian and gay marriages is unclear, however.

When invading Europeans and Americans overturned native cultures in modern times, they spread European homophobia through law codes and missionary preaching. The exposure to Christianity and the desire to appear "civilized" have influenced the treatment of homosexuals in many non-Western cultures. In some places, such as most of Africa, populations have become more hostile to homosexuality than had their former colonizers.

Jewish interpretation of these texts was that homosexual behavior contradicted God's law.

Genesis 2:18–24 tells the second of two creation stories in the Bible. In this version, God creates woman (Eve) from one of Adam's ribs because "it is not good for man to be alone." The Bible concludes the story by stating, "Hence a man leaves his father and mother and clings to his wife, so that they become one flesh." From this text, some commentators interpret the ideal relationship (and marriage) to be exclusively heterosexual and monogamous.

Parts of the Bible seem to imply that marriage exclusively involves one man and one woman. However, the Bible does not forbid a man from having multiple wives, and examples of polygamy in the Bible pass without comment. Abraham had concubines (Genesis 25:6), Rehoboam had eighteen wives and sixty concubines (2 Chronicles 11:21) and Solomon, supposedly the wisest of men, had seven hundred wives and three hundred concubines (2 Kings 11:3).

The section on homosexuality in Leviticus 20:13 states, "If a man lies with a male as one lies with a woman, the two of them have done an abhorrent thing ("an abomination" in some translations); they shall be put to death—their bloodguilt is upon them." Religious conservatives generally interpret this verse straightforwardly: anal sex between two males (no mention is made of lesbian or oral sex) is "abhorrent," and the prescribed penalty is death. On the other hand, liberal Jews interpret this section narrowly, as applying only to male Jews who engaged in same-sex rituals in pagan temples. According to this view, the verse's concern was with ritual purity and religious taboos, not the morality of the sex itself.

The Bible story of the destruction of the cities of Sodom and Gomorrah (Genesis 19:4–5) is also contested ground between supporters and opponents of same-sex marriage. The traditional reading interprets this famous chapter as describing God's wrath against the homosexual desires of the male population of the two cities. The word *sodomite* derives from the name of the city in the story, and the most common definition of that word refers to someone who engages in anal sex. In contrast, certain modern biblical scholars believe that the sin of Sodom was the population's lack of hospitality and not homosexuality. In this view, the moral of the story is that it is wrong to mistreat strangers, widows, and travelers.

Present-day Jews hold a wide range of opinions toward same-sex marriage. Orthodox Judaism—the most conservative of the three main branches of Judaism, strictly applying laws and ethics predating the Middle Ages—views homosexuality as a sinful choice and does not accept same-sex relationships. Although the Bible makes no clear mention of lesbian sex, rabbinical writers forbade female homosexuality largely on the basis of Deuteronomy 22:5. One Orthodox rabbi declared, "It is impossible for Judaism to make peace with homosexuality because homosexuality denies many of Judaism's most fundamental values."

The Conservative branch of Judaism follows traditional Jewish law but believes it can evolve to meet the changing ethical realities of modern life. Conservative Jews have debated the issue of homosexuality since the 1990s. In 2006, a panel of Conservative rabbis gave permission for same-sex commitment ceremonies. The decision, which gave individual rabbis the option of blessing same-sex unions, provoked a great deal of opposition in many Conservative congregations. By the next year, however, the Jewish Theological Seminary, the main institution of Conservative Judaism, had begun accepting applicants who were in same-sex relationships.

Reform Judaism, the largest branch of Judaism in the United States, rejects the word-for-word application of traditional Jewish law and advocates using its rules as guidelines rather than morally binding restrictions. The Reform leadership has allowed its rabbis to perform same-sex commitment ceremonies since 2000. Reform Jews generally believe either that traditional laws against homosexuality are no longer binding or that they are subject to changes that reflect a new understanding of human sexuality. One rabbi said, "I do not believe that God creates in vain. Deep, heartfelt yearning for companionship and intimacy is not an abomination before God."

Many advocates of same-sex marriage have noted that the Bible accepts slavery (Leviticus 25:44–46) and prescribes the death penalty for numerous sins including gathering wood on the Sabbath (Numbers 15:32–36) and insulting one's parents (Leviticus 20:9). Even the most traditional Jews have modified or interpreted away these strictures. Yet not all are willing to do the same with regard to marriage. "Discarding the historical definition of marriage would pose a severe danger to society," said an Orthodox Jewish organization. "That prospect is chilling, and should be unacceptable."

Catholicism

The Christian Gospels (the books of Matthew, Mark, Luke, and John) have relatively little to say about sex. Some have interpreted the silence to mean Jesus was not particularly interested in the subject. He spoke at far greater length on subjects such as the evils of wealth and demonic possession.

After the death of Jesus, the early Christian church decided that Jewish law was not binding on Christians. Christians rejected Jewish dietary laws (such as the prohibitions against pork and shellfish) and the distinctive ritual ceremony of circumcision (a central requirement of Jewish law). Most Christians considered the Jewish Bible, which they called the Old Testament, to be a prelude to Christian revelation. Its moral or legal force was subject to limits. In Catholic tradition, although the Old Testament's ceremonial requirements are no longer applicable, its moral requirements are eternal and binding upon all cultures.

The Apostle Paul's letters in the New Testament of the Christian Bible show far greater concern with sexual issues than the Gospels. Paul generally considered any kind of sex—homosexual or heterosexual—a major source of sin and an obstacle to a truly Christian life. The only texts from the New Testament that mention homosexuality at any length are Paul's letters to the Romans (1:18–33) and to the Corinthians (the second one, 6:1–11), as well as a similar text in 1 Timothy (1:9–10).

The letter to the Romans is widely read today as a clear criticism of homosexuality. It includes this passage: "For this reason God gave them up to degrading passions. Their women exchanged natural intercourse for unnatural, and in the same way also the men, giving up natural intercourse with women, were consumed with passion for one another. Men committed shameless acts with men and received in their own persons the due penalty for their error." Gay Catholics, however, claim that Paul used the phrase "unnatural intercourse" to refer to excessive indulgence in sex and not homosexuality.

In 1 Corinthians, Paul wrote, "Do you not know that wrongdoers will not inherit the kingdom of God? Do not be deceived! Fornicators, idolaters, adulterers, male prostitutes (*malakoi*), sodomites (*arsenokoitai*), thieves, the greedy, drunkards, revilers, robbers—none of these will inherit the kingdom of God." A sizable dispute exists about what precisely the Greek words refer to and how to translate them.

Human sexuality remains an area of conflict for Catholic theologians. In spite of the positive view of physical love found in the Old Testament Song of Songs and despite God's command to Adam and Eve to "go forth and multiply" (Genesis 1:28), Catholic writers have historically viewed sex unenthusiastically. Opponents of Christianity say that this attitude is not surprising for a religion whose founder was supposed to have no biological father, who is believed to have no siblings, and who never married. Early Christians viewed marriage and sexual intercourse as unavoidable, since it was needed to continue the human race. Homosexual and heterosexual acts were opposed to each other, but both were opposed

The Bible is cited by many—not all of them members of religious sects—as a reason to condemn homosexuality. Charles Lee (center), a Ku Klux Klan Grand Dragon, was one of a handful of protestors screaming abuse at gay couples in Houston, Texas, as the couples protested the Defense of Marriage Act.

to the higher (that is, closer to the ideal) state: chastity. For at least a thousand years, the Church placed a higher value on priestly celibacy, voluntary virginity (even for the married), and monastic community life than on sexual activity within the family unit.

In the twenty-first century, the Catholic Church has continued to be a staunch opponent of same-sex marriage. This statement, issued by the National Conference of Catholic Bishops in 1996, presents the essential Roman Catholic position:

The Roman Catholic Church believes that marriage is a faithful, exclusive, and lifelong union between one man and one woman, joined as husband and wife in an intimate partnership of life and love. This union was established by God with its own proper laws . . . marriage exists for the mutual love and support of the spouses and for the procreation and education of children. These two purposes, the unitive and the procreative, are equal and inseparable. . . . Thus, we oppose attempts to grant the legal status of marriage to a relationship between persons of the same sex. No same-sex union can realize the unique and full potential which the marital relationship expresses.

As a result, the Catholic Church has urged its members to work against same-sex marriage. "Where homosexual unions have been legally recognized . . . clear and emphatic opposition is a duty," wrote Cardinal Joseph Ratzinger in 2003. "One must refrain from any kind of formal cooperation in the enactment or application of such gravely unjust laws. . . . In this area, everyone can exercise the right to conscientious objection." In 2005, Ratzinger was elected pope as Benedict XVI.

Catholic supporters of same-sex marriage complain about what they term the selective analysis of the texts and the disproportionate response of the Church. Jesus condemned divorce and remarriage in far stronger terms (Mark 10:9–11), and Catholics are forbidden to use birth control. This censure has not stopped Catholics from divorcing and using contraceptives, yet the Pope does not ask Catholics to "refrain from any kind of formal cooperation" with liberal divorce laws. No Catholic leaders suggest that the government should not issue marriage licenses to divorced couples or even to divorced Catholic couples.

Protestantism

Protestants, also Christians, do not have a church hierarchy topped by the pope, as Catholics do. One of the basic principles of Protestantism is the right of people to read and interpret the Bible in the light of their own understanding. As a result, numerous Protestant denominations exist, each with its own interpretations of religious and social issues. It is not surprising, then, that there is no single Protestant response to homosexuality and same-sex marriage. Some Protestants note that the Bible depicts man-lying-with-man as an "abomination"; others say the main message of the Bible is God's love for all people, who are created in God's image.

A number of Protestant groups have taken a hard line against same-sex marriage. Southern Baptists condemn homosexuality as a sin; their 2003 convention affirmed that "legal and biblical marriage can only occur between one man and one woman." For this reason, Southern Baptists declare that they "oppose steadfastly all efforts by any court or state legislature to validate or legalize same-sex marriage or other equivalent unions." The convention called on all Southern Baptists "to stand against same-sex unions." This opposition is important, because Southern Baptists are the largest Protestant body in the United States with more than 16 million members and 42,000 churches.

In 2005, on the other hand, the United Church of Christ became the largest Christian denomination in the United States to endorse same-sex marriage. The church, with about a million members in the United States, endorsed "local, state, and national legislation to grant equal marriage rights to couples regardless of gender, and to work against legislation, including constitutional amendments, which denies civil marriage rights to couples based on gender."

Some Protestant denominations have been split by the controversy. For example, Sweden's Lutheran church—the largest Lutheran group in the world, with more than 6 million members—became the first major Protestant church to conduct gay weddings.

The church's decision followed legislation passed by the Swedish parliament allowing homosexuals to marry. Yet the Lutheran Church–Missouri Synod, with more than 2 million members, re-affirmed its position that homosexual behavior is sinful and that same-sex marriage is "contrary to the will of the Creator."

Islam

Of all the major religions, modern-day Islam is probably the one most uncompromisingly opposed to same-sex marriage and homo-sexuality. Islam draws its doctrines from the Jewish and Christian Scriptures, as well as from the Koran, or Qur'an—the collection of the writings of Muhammad—which supersedes them. In general, conservatives in these three religions interpret the major scriptural passages the same way. All major Islamic sects disapprove of ho-mosexuality and consider it a transgression, a departure from the natural order of sexual activity. There are some Islamic dissenters but far fewer as a total percentage of believers than may be found in Christianity and Judaism.

In addition to the already cited texts in the Jewish and Chris-tian Bibles, Muslims opposed to same-sex marriage cite several verses in the Qur'an, 7:80–81, and a similar text in 26:165–166: "We also selected Lüt, who said to his people: 'Will you do such indecent acts as no one else in the world has committed before you? You satisfy your lust with men instead of women. Indeed you are a nation that has transgressed beyond bounds.'"

The sharia (traditional Islamic law) explicitly denounces ho-mosexuality and same-sex marriage; Islamic scholars disagree only on the severity of punishment for what are termed sinful and per-verted acts. Many countries with a majority of Muslims do not separate church and state. The majority of these countries—rang-ing from the "liberal" country of Tunisia to the dictatorship of Sudan—outlaw same-sex relationships. As of 2010, seven sharia-governed countries assigned the death penalty to persons found

Clergy and lay members of the Episcopal diocese of San Joaquin, California, split with the national denomination over disagreements about the role of gays and lesbians in the church. In 2007, this became the first full diocese to secede — over gay rights.

Anglicans at War with Each Other

The issue of homosexuality and same-sex marriage has torn apart the Anglican Church, a major Protestant group with more than 70 million members (most American Anglicans are members of one of several Episcopalian denominations). Traditionalist Anglicans are strongly opposed to the ordination of gay clergy and the blessing of same-sex relationships, while liberals urge tolerance and change. Not all Anglican churches have to agree on every issue in order to call themselves Anglican. However, the question of gay ordinations and same-sex marriage seem to have stretched the notion of a common faith past the breaking point.

In general, the Asian and African Anglican churches (except the South African one) condemn homosexuality as sinful. The West African Anglican Archbishop called homosexuality "unscriptural, unnatural, and totally incompatible with Christian values." The Nigerian Anglican Church, with 15 million members, officially committed itself to "the total rejection of the evil of homosexuality which is a perversion of human dignity. . . ." In arguing for the passage of a bill barring same-sex marriage, the Nigerian Anglican Church declared that "same-sex marriage is out to foist on the world a false sense of the family, which will bring disastrous consequences to mankind . . . [it is] a perversion, a deviation and an aberration that is capable of engendering moral and social holocaust in this country. Outlawing it is to ensure the continued existence of this nation."

On the other hand, North American Anglican churches have been more open to ordaining homosexuals and performing same-sex marriages. The American Episcopal Church ordained an openly gay bishop in 2003 and began blessing same-sex unions. In 2006, the church stated its "support of gay and lesbian persons and [opposition to] any state or federal constitutional amendment that prohibits same-sex marriages or unions." In 2010, the Los Angeles diocese of the Episcopal Church ordained an openly lesbian bishop, an action that further increased tensions. As of 2011, the strife within the Anglican community dividing supporters and opponents of same-sex marriage remained unresolved.

Not all Christians are against gay rights; some Protestant sects are inclusive.

guilty of homosexual acts. In these countries many people view same-sex marriage as an import from Western culture and an indication of its moral weakness.

Some Muslim organizations in America have been active in opposing same-sex marriage. The Islamic Shura Council, a large organization of mosques and Muslim groups in Southern California, called same-sex marriages "a violation of God's law as clearly given in the Qur'an and the Bible." The group said that same-sex marriages "will corrode the very structure of society. . . . Marriage in Islam is defined as a man and a woman coming together under God to form a family to promote and perpetuate life. . . ."

This position notwithstanding, Islam permits polygamy; men are permitted to have up to four wives.

The Church of Jesus Christ of Latter-day Saints

The Church of Jesus Christ of Latter-day Saints (LDS)—commonly referred to as the Mormon Church—has become one of the driving forces in the opposition to gay marriage in the United States. The LDS insists that it does not oppose civil unions or other limited rights for same-sex couples. However, according to an official LDS pronouncement, "The Church's teachings and position on this moral issue are unequivocal. Marriage between a man and a woman is ordained of God, and the formation of families is central to the Creator's plan for His children."

In California, LDS members worked hard to pass Proposition 8, which banned same-sex marriage in the state. An LDS Church directive called same-sex marriage "one of the great moral issues of our time." It asked members to "do all you can to support the proposed constitutional amendment by donating of your means and time to assure that marriage in California is legally defined as being between a man and a woman. Our best efforts are required to preserve the sacred institution of marriage."

As the LDS Church achieved a higher profile in the fight against same-sex marriage, it came under attack from gay rights supporters. A 2010 movie documentary called *8: The Mormon Proposition*, claimed that the LDS Church overstepped its bounds as a nonprofit religious organization in order to ensure that Proposition 8 passed. "The people in California went to the ballot box with misinformation and lies orchestrated by billions of dollars raised by a church," asserted one of the filmmakers.

The LDS did not back down. Its officials defended "speaking out against practices with which the Church disagrees on moral grounds—including same-sex marriage. . . . We can express genuine love and friendship for the homosexual family member or friend without accepting the practice of homosexuality or any redefinition of marriage."

Not all the rhetoric was so civil. Chris Buttars, a Mormon state representative from Utah, told the press that gays and lesbians were "the greatest threat to America going down" and compared homosexuals to radical Muslims. "I believe they will destroy the foundation of the American society," he said. "In my mind, it's the beginning of the end. . . . Sodom and Gomorrah was localized. This is worldwide."

Indian Religions

Historically, the religions that originated in India, including Hinduism, Buddhism, Jainism, and Sikhism, were ambivalent regarding homosexuality. Most contemporary authorities in these religions view homosexuality negatively. It is usually discouraged or actively forbidden.

Many ancient Hindu law books classify both female and male homosexuality as impure and a punishable crime. In a 2004 survey, most swamis (Hindu religious teachers) said they opposed the concept of a Hindu-sanctified gay marriage. One swami told *Hinduism Today*, "Gay marriages do not fit with our culture and heritage. All those people who are raising demand for approving such marriages in India are doing so under the influence of the West . . . we do not even discuss it."

However, the nature of the Hindu religion allows followers to form their own opinions. A Hindu priest in India who performed a wedding for two women in 2002 concluded, based on Hindu scriptures, that "marriage is a union of spirits, and the spirit is not male or female." There are more than a million Hindus in the United States, and members of the same temple often have varying opinions.

In general, Buddhist sects do not make definitive claims on right and wrong in the everyday activities of life, although it is a basic Buddhist principle that a person should renounce sensual pleasure. Because of the ambiguous language toward homosexuality found in Buddhist teachings, there is no official position on the issue of same-sex marriage. Buddhist scriptures warn against "sexual misconduct," but the term is broad; its definition usually depends on the social norms of the followers. Buddhists in Europe and North America show a growing moral acceptance of same-sex sexual activity. In Thailand, Cambodia, and other Asian countries with large Buddhist populations, most people disapprove of homosexuality and same-sex marriage.

Sikhism is the fifth largest religion in the world, and as of 2010, about a half-million Sikhs live in the United States. The Sikh religion also has no definitive written view regarding same-sex marriage. In 2005, a high-ranking Sikh religious authority called on Sikhs in Canada to fight same-sex marriage legislation. Saying that the idea of same-sex marriages originated from sick minds, he condemned homosexuality as "against the Sikh religion and the Sikh code of conduct and totally against the laws of nature." One Sikh legislator in Canada countered that the Sikh emphasis on human rights and tolerance, particularly for marginalized and persecuted groups, make it an obligation to support same-sex marriage.

Religious Dissent to Same-Sex Unions

Same-sex-marriage supporters argue that their movement is not about forcing any religious institution to change any of its views or beliefs. Catholics, Mormons, and Orthodox Jews cannot be compelled to celebrate religious ceremonies they do not believe in. "This civil rights movement is about equal legal rights, not diverse religious rites," said one advocate.

However, in places where same-sex marriage is legal, some religious people face a crisis of conscience. Since many states have laws prohibiting discrimination based on sexual orientation, business-owning opponents of same-sex marriage might not have a legal right to refuse to provide services for same-sex weddings, even if doing so would violate their own religious beliefs. This prohibition might extend to people who work in the registrar's office, as well as to reception-hall owners, photographers, bakers, caterers, and florists. For example, the Iowa attorney general told county recorders that they must issue licenses to same-sex couples. New Mexico's Human Rights Commission fined a photography studio that refused to photograph a same-sex commitment ceremony. The New Jersey government removed the property-tax exemption of a church group that denied requests by two lesbian couples to use the group's boardwalk pavilion for their commitment ceremonies.

Most countries and states that have passed same-sex marriage laws have included some sort of conscience-protection clause for religious dissenters. These laws usually state that religious groups do not have to provide services, accommodations, facilities, or goods to an individual if the request relates to the solemnization of a marriage or celebration of a marriage. These laws also exempt religious organizations from granting same-sex partners spousal benefits. In 2010, for example, Catholic Charities of Washington, D.C., limited employee health-care benefits for spouses to opposite-sex couples.

There are limits to the exemption, however. Once a state recognizes a marriage, same-sex-marriage supporters argue, all discrimination in housing, employment, adoption, and similar areas should be illegal. Religious groups should not have the right to apply religious criteria to activities outside their faith tradition. Same-sex and opposite-sex married couples should be treated alike. Conscience protection, say supporters, also should not exempt photographers or florists from providing their services. When individuals enter the commercial market as employers or sellers, they limit their freedom of action. If a catering hall hosts wedding receptions for opposite-sex couples, it must also do so for gays and lesbians. Opponents of same-sex marriage, however, argue that this policy infringes on the First Amendment right of freedom of religion.

4 **Procreation and Children**

OPPONENTS OF SAME-SEX MARRIAGE OFTEN USE what might be called the "basic-biology argument." This argument can take several forms. The first states that homosexual relations deny the self-evident truth that male and female bodies complement each other. "Redefining the natural and divine institution of marriage is simply something we are not able to do," said one Catholic priest in California. "From all time, it is obvious, for the species to procreate, it requires a man and a woman. The bodies are made to fit with each other."

Opponents also argue that marriage between a man and a woman is unique in that it alone permits procreation. "The ancient definition of marriage as the union of one man and one woman has its basis in biology, not bigotry," an American judge wrote. "The fact that same sex couples cannot engage in sexual conduct of a type that can result in the birth of a child is a critical difference in this context."

The basic-biology argument culminates in the claim that children do better in life if they are raised by a mother and a father. Therefore, it is in the government's interest to promote such an arrangement by restricting marriage to opposite-sex couples. "The government of a state is entitled to declare what is and is not normal family structure," said one opponent of same-sex marriage. The LDS Church stated the problem in more dire terms: "The legalization of same-sex marriage likely will erode the social identity,

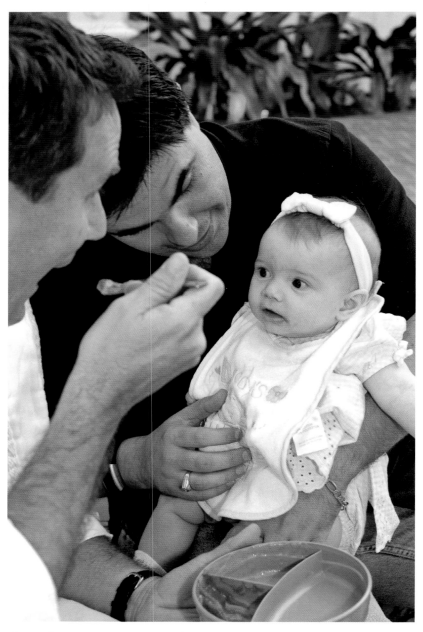

Those who oppose gay marriage often cite the basic-biology argument: same-sex couples cannot bear children. Yet in most of the United States, gays can legally adopt the many children whose biological parents can't or choose not to raise them.

gender development, and moral character of children. Is it really wise for society to pursue such a radical experiment without taking into account its long-term consequences for children?"

In the twenty-first century, however, the argument cuts both ways. Using artificial insemination, in vitro fertilization, and surrogate motherhood, thousands of same-sex (and opposite sex) couples are raising kids. This is an age where an ovum can be fertilized on a glass slide. Lesbians can get pregnant and bear children, and gay men are as capable as other men of providing sperm to inseminate a woman. Although precise numbers are hard to come by, the number of lesbians using artificial reproductive technology to have children appears to be rising. This may not be "basic" biology, but advocates say that it undercuts the claim that there is something uniquely procreative about monogamous, heterosexual marriage.

In addition, rising numbers of Americans are having children without being married. Nearly 40 percent of babies born in the United States in 2007 were delivered by unwed mothers; a record 1.7 million out-of-wedlock births out of 4.3 million total births. Encouraging this trend might not be good public policy, since children born to unwed parents face a greater likelihood of being poor and of becoming high school dropouts. Yet the existence of almost 10 million single mothers and 2 million single fathers in the United States seems to break the link between marriage and procreation. If basic biology leads to procreation, it certainly does not lead inevitably to marriage.

Procreation and Family

Does changing the definition of who can get married have an impact on procreation and children? In ballot initiatives and court cases, supporters and opponents have used the testimony of psychologists, historians, and social scientists to support their positions.

Some opponents of same-sex marriage have argued that the main or even the sole purpose of marriage is procreation. "Marriage was founded to propagate the species," said one opponent of same-sex marriage." Two individuals of the same gender, whatever their affections, can never form a marriage devoted to raising their own mutual offspring. One U.S. senator declared that it was "common sense that a marriage is between a man and a woman. Marriage is not about affirming somebody's love for somebody else," he claimed. "It's about uniting together to be open to children, to further civilization in our society."

This argument carries little weight with supporters of same-sex marriage. Couples have many reasons to marry besides producing children: love, companionship, mutual caring and support, personal commitment, and even sometimes economics. Every state government in the United States routinely issues marriage licenses to elderly, sterile, and impotent couples. No state requires straight couples to prove that they can procreate or promise that they will procreate before issuing a marriage license. Why then raise the objection when gay couples want to marry?

For several decades, states have also permitted gay couples to adopt children as well as conceive them through reproductive technologies such as in vitro fertilization. Of the thirteen plaintiff couples in the same-sex-marriage cases in Hawaii, Vermont, and Massachusetts, six were parents, with a total of seven children. The eight Connecticut same-sex couples in *Kerrigan* v. *Commissioner of Public Health* had fourteen children among them.

In the *Goodridge* case (2003), same-sex-marriage opponents argued that marriage's primary purpose was procreation. The Massachusetts Supreme Court rejected the argument. "That is not correct," the court said. Marriage laws "contain no requirement that applicants for a marriage license attest to their ability or intention to conceive a child by coitus. Fertility is not a condition of marriage, nor is it grounds for divorce. . . . Even people who cannot stir from their deathbed may marry." The court concluded, "While it is certainly true that many, perhaps most, married couples have

People get married for all sorts of reasons these days, including couples who are far too old to have children.

children together (assisted or unassisted), it is the exclusive and permanent commitment of the marriage partners to one another, not the begetting of children, that is the sine qua non [that is, the essential condition] of civil marriage."

However, in *Andersen* v. *King County* (2006), the Washington Supreme Court thought otherwise. The court ruled that the state's mini–DOMA was constitutional because "limiting marriage to opposite-sex couples furthers procreation, essential to the survival of the human race, and furthers the well-being of children by encouraging families where children are reared in homes headed by the children's biological parents." Dissenters argued that even if this were true, it was not clear how giving same-sex couples the right to marry would harm the state's interest in procreation and healthy child rearing.

U.S. Supreme Court Justice Antonin Scalia, a vehement opponent of same-sex marriage, noted the weakness of the procreation argument. In his dissent in *Lawrence* v. *Texas*, he argued that moral disapproval should be sufficient grounds for the government to ban homosexual conduct. Otherwise, "what justification could there possibly be for denying the benefits of marriage to homosexual couples? Surely not the encouragement of procreation, since the sterile and the elderly are allowed to marry."

Other same-sex-marriage opponents are not willing to surrender the procreation argument so easily. "Exceptions do not invalidate a norm or the necessity of norms," wrote one. "How some individuals make use of marriage . . . does not determine the purpose of that institution." The LDS Church made a similar argument by linking the sacred nature of marriage to the power of procreation. "It is true that some couples who marry will not have children, either by choice or because of infertility," admitted the Church. Nonetheless, the special status of marriage is "closely linked to the inherent powers and responsibilities of procreation, and to the inherent differences between the genders."

The sexual union of men and women has usually been associated with certain legal protections and often has been given a special status because such unions result in children. If procreation is no longer a crucial element of marriage, then marriage becomes just another private relationship in which society and the government have no special interest. For some same-sex-marriage supporters, this state of affairs is as it should be. They wish to place limits on the government's power to regulate marriage. However, civil marriage in Europe and the United States is so well established and so popular that it seems unlikely that the state will relinquish its role as a regulator of marriage anytime soon.

A bit of dialogue from a same-sex marriage court case in California in 2009 sums up the problematic nature of linking marriage to procreation. The lawsuit claimed that California's voters violated the federal Constitution in 2008 when they overrode a decision of the state's supreme court allowing same-sex marriages. Charles Cooper, the attorney for the defendants, argued that the government should be allowed to favor opposite-sex marriages in order "to channel naturally procreative sexual activity between men and women into stable, enduring unions."

Judge Vaughn Walker appeared puzzled. "The last marriage that I performed," the judge said, "involved a groom who was 95, and the bride was 83. I did not demand that they prove that they intended to engage in procreative activity. Now, was I missing something?"

Mr. Cooper said no.

"And I might say it was a very happy relationship," Judge Walker said.

"I rejoice to hear that," Mr. Cooper responded, and then returned to his theme that only procreation matters in marriage. A few hours later, Judge Walker denied Cooper's motion to dismiss the lawsuit, which sought to establish a constitutional right to same-sex marriage.

65

Natural Law

Both advocates and opponents of same-sex marriage make appeals to nature to bolster their arguments. The basic-biology argument frames same-sex marriage as unnatural. The Catholic Church often uses this interpretation by referring to natural law in discussing what it calls sins against nature. "People have a basic, ethical intuition that certain behaviors are wrong because they are unnatural," argued Cardinal Joseph Ratzinger before he was elected Pope Benedict XVI. "We perceive intuitively that the natural sex partner of a human is another human, not an animal. The same reasoning applies to the case of homosexual behavior." Therefore, homosexuality is wrong because it is unnatural.

Ratzinger, then a cardinal, stated the official Catholic position in 2003. "There are absolutely no grounds for considering homosexual unions to be in any way similar or even remotely analogous to God's plan for marriage and family," he said. "Marriage is holy, while homosexual acts go against the natural moral law. . . . Under no circumstances can they be approved."

The widespread presence of homosexual activity in nature creates problems for this argument. Scientists have observed the pairing of same-sex couples in more than a thousand species, including penguins, dolphins, and many types of primates. Some scientists, noting that some of these same-sex-animal unions are long lasting, think they may be beneficial to the survival of the species.

If this is the case, then perhaps the reverse of the natural-law argument is true, and the natural world actually makes a case for the acceptance of homosexuality in humans. Supporters of this view have argued that because human beings are products of the natural world, they should mimic behavior seen in the natural world. If homosexuality is found in nature, it must be "natural."

For still others, an appeal to nature is not a strong argument for anything. Some things found in nature are not particularly beneficial (earthquakes, leukemia) or even generally accepted according to human morality (having sexual relations with siblings; parents killing their offspring). Some unnatural things have extremely desirable properties—things like antibiotics and electric lights. In addition, it is an open question if it is useful or even logical to use animal behavior to justify what is or is not moral. Reading human motivations and sentiments into animal behavior can make for shaky science and ethics.

Same-Sex Parenting

A common objection to gay marriage involves the welfare of children. "If it were not for kids, I would have no problem whatsoever with gay marriage," said one California resident. Children need both a father and a mother to thrive, he explained. "That's the ideal, and that's what should be upheld. . . . To purposely start without one of the sexes makes it worse on a kid." Massachusetts state representative Eugene L. O'Flaherty agreed. He listed the reasons he opposed same-sex marriage: "procreation, family stability, the preservation of the family as a social unit, and studies showing that children do better when raised by a father and a mother."

Still, in many places legislation regulating adoption has already made same-sex couples and single gay, lesbian, and heterosexual people eligible to adopt. Most states in the United States allow gay and lesbian couples to adopt children; as of 2010, only Florida prohibited lesbians and gay men from adopting children. Adoption by same-sex couples is legal in many European countries, including the United Kingdom, Norway, Spain, the Netherlands, and Sweden.

In 2008, the European Court of Human Rights overturned French court rulings that prevented a single lesbian woman from adopting a child. The decision essentially set a precedent that same-sex couples throughout most of Europe had the right to adopt a child. Adoptive parents may not be involved in procreation, but they are involved in child-rearing and so have the same legal concerns as parents who conceive children in the traditional way. The consensus of America's leading child welfare and health organizations is that a parent's sexual orientation has nothing to do with his or her ability to be a good parent. Many of these groups have condemned discrimination based on sexual orientation in adoption and child custody. A position paper by the American Psychological Association also supported adoption by same-sex couples: Numerous studies over the last three decades demonstrate that children raised by gay or lesbian parents exhibit the same level of emotional, cognitive, social, and sexual functioning as children raised by heterosexual parents. This research indicates that optimal development for children is based, not on the sexual orientation of the parents, but on stable attachments to committed and nurturing adults. The research also shows that children who have two parents, regardless of the parents' sexual orientations, do better than children with only one parent.

The Canadian Department of Justice came to a similar conclusion in 2006. "[T]he vast majority of studies show that children living with two mothers and children living with a mother and father have the same levels of social competence," their report read. "A few studies suggest that children with two lesbian mothers may have marginally better social competence than children in traditional nuclear families, even fewer studies show the opposite, and most studies fail to find any differences."

Opponents of same-sex marriage are not convinced. "Children do best when raised by their own biological mother and father who are committed to one another in a lifelong marriage." However, this supposedly normative household is not prevalent in the United States. Almost half of all American heterosexual marriages end in divorce, and millions of children are not living with their biological parents. In 2010, so-called traditional families (married couples with their own children) made up only about one in five American households. At the same time, the number of unmarried couples living together increased tenfold; about 10 million people (8 percent of U.S. coupled households) are cohabiting with a partner of the opposite sex.

In fact, research does not indicate that children do better with a mother and a father. Instead, it seems to show that children generally do better with two parents regardless of gender. The quality of parenting depends less on gender than on love, commitment, responsibility, and self-sacrifice. Child psychiatrist Kyle Pruett, director of medical studies at Yale University's Child Study Center, said

While those against gay marriage argue that children do best with a biological mother and father, an increasing number of children in today's United States are being raised by one parent.

that theoretically "it is best to have a mother and father who are biologically connected and who[m] the state supports in raising the child. But once you move from the theoretical to the practical, it is the quality of the relationship that children have with their parents that is far more determinative of their eventual life outcome."

This research has not swayed everyone. People who believe homosexuality is a choice, and a sinful one at that, fear that children nurtured by gay parents are more likely to become gay themselves. The LDS Church stated, "Traditional marriage provides a solid and well-established social identity to children. It increases the likelihood that they will be able to form a clear gender identity, with sexuality closely linked to both love and procreation." Others make this argument more broadly. The president of the Institute for American Values testified in federal court that he opposed same-sex marriage because heterosexual marriages serve as "seed beds from which come good citizens" who are more likely to contribute to society.

Punishing the Kids?

In reality, a considerable number of American children—as of 2005, about 270,000—already live in families headed by gay men or lesbians. (This number included an estimated 65,000 adopted children living with gay or lesbian parents.) Because homosexuals are already parents in large numbers, say supporters, it would be better for those children to be protected in their families by legal marriage rather than live with instability and possible custodial problems. One advocate said, "There is no good reason to punish children raised by gay parents by denying parents marriage and its protections. It harms kids rather than helping them."

Same-sex-marriage supporters argue that all children deserve to know that their relationships with both of their parents are stable and legally recognized. They cite a report by the American Academy of Pediatrics that recognized "when two adults participate in parenting a child, they and the child deserve the serenity that comes with legal recognition."

Opponents challenge this argument. "It doesn't make any sense that a small segment of society can leverage major social change simply by putting children into these situations purposefully," argued one. "Society is not forcing same-sex parents to raise children. If they are going to exercise their choice, it remains their choice and not become something that society has to realign itself to accept."

Schools

If a state legalizes same-sex marriage, will schools teach that gay and straight relationships are equal? The thought horrifies many socially conservative Americans. Arguing for the passage of Proposition 8 in California, supporters specifically argued that the proposition "*protects our children* from being taught in public schools that 'same-sex marriage' is the same as traditional marriage."

This argument turned out to be particularly effective in winning passage of Proposition 8. "If the gay marriage ruling is not overturned, teachers could be required to teach young children there is *no difference* between gay marriage and traditional marriage," argued backers. "We should not accept a court decision that may result in public schools teaching our kids that gay marriage is okay."

The schooling argument had wide resonance. Conservatives did not want schoolchildren to be taught that marriage was a relationship between any two adults and that consensual sexual relations were morally neutral. They feared the undermining of the rights of parents to teach their children traditional standards of morality.

Same-sex-marriage supporters attempted to respond. "Don't be tricked by scare tactics," they wrote. "Prop. 8 doesn't have anything to do with schools . . . local school districts and parents—not the state—develop health education programs for their schools."

At the same time, advocates for gay marriage have tried to turn the family-values argument on its head by playing their own "child card." They have used articulate children raised by same-sex parents to project a "mainstream" family image in public-opinion campaigns. These children appear in advertisements and public hearings asking why their families should have fewer rights than their neighbors. For example, a ten-year-old boy told the New Jersey State Senate, "It doesn't bother me to tell kids my parents are gay. It does bother me to say they aren't married. It makes me feel that our family is less than their family."

Arguing "for the sake of the children" has been attacked widely and vehemently. One Cincinnati newspaper columnist complained, "It's always the same story. There's a photo of a loving, caring, monogamous lesbian couple, raising adopted orphans. 'We only want the rights given to everyone else,' they plead. So the definition of marriage that has outlasted the Great Pyramids and crosses more cultural, geographic, religious and ethnic boundaries than the Great Wall of China is crumbling under the slow drip of 'I want.'"

Lifestyle Choice or Genetic Predisposition?

A basic conceptual issue in the debate over same-sex marriage is the nature of same-sex eroticism. Many people consider being gay a lifestyle choice. This position is often (not always) associated with same-sex marriage opponents, especially those who see homosexuality as a sin or a misguided choice. They see homosexuality stemming from a variety of causes: poor parenting, psychiatric problems, sexual molestation during childhood, improper cultural influences. They want to fight any efforts to treat homosexuality as a natural practice to prevent more young people from experimenting with it and becoming trapped in the lifestyle.

Many who support gay rights believe that homosexuality is not a matter of taste or choice. They think gays are people who live their lives, just as heterosexuals do, with a sexual orientation fixed at birth or at an early age. They argue that while science has not authoritatively determined how sexual orientation is formed, for most people it is a matter of neither casual choice nor upbringing. One Episcopalian bishop supported same-sex marriage because "a homosexual orientation is a minority but perfectly natural characteristic on the human spectrum of sexuality. It is not something one chooses, it is something one is. . . ." To many gay rights activists, the attempt to "explain" homosexuality is a subtle way to label it an illness in need of treatment.

The controversy over the origins of same-sex eroticism is beyond the present volume's scope. It is enough to note that the belief that homosexuality is a choice has definite ramifications. If homosexuality is a choice, the relationship between same-sex marriage and civil rights becomes shaky; there would be a major difference between same-sex marriage and interracial marriage. Same-sex-marriage opponents assert that, in general, race and ethnicity are categories that cannot be chosen and involve no moral choices. These claims cannot be made for homosexuality.

Also, opponents who believe that homosexuality is a choice, and a bad one at that, argue that because parents affect a child's sexual orientation, kids raised by gay parents will be swayed toward becoming gay. Those who do not will be disturbed by the presence of homosexuality in the home. The future Pope Benedict XVI wrote in 2003 that secular governments "need to contain the phenomenon within certain limits so as to safeguard public morality and, above all, to avoid exposing young people to erroneous ideas about sexuality and marriage that would deprive them of their necessary defenses and contribute to the spread of the phenomenon."

Not all opponents accept this premise, however. In 1978, the people of California defeated a referendum to exclude gay people from schoolteaching, the contention being that they would be bad role models. Ronald Reagan, then the governor of California and a noted conservative voice, worked to defeat it. Reagan wrote in one editorial, "Whatever else it is, homosexuality is not a contagious disease like the measles. Prevailing scientific opinion is that a child's teachers do not really influence this." He humorously concluded, "As to the role model argument, a woman writing to the editor of a Southern California newspaper said it all: "If teachers had such power over children, I would have been a nun years ago.'"

5 The Civil Rights Debate

ONE OF THE MOST WIDELY HEARD ARGUMENTS IN support of same-sex marriage is a rhetorical question: "How would it harm someone to allow others to marry?" Same-sex marriage is essentially harmless, say its supporters; it will not affect traditional heterosexual marriage in any way. "The claim that same-sex marriage will deter heterosexual marriage seems to me implausible," argued one libertarian conservative. "I just can't see a likely mechanism for it. It would seem odd that the permission of same-sex marriages among the approximately 3 percent of the population that is homosexual would materially affect the behavior of the remaining 97 percent."

Opponents continue to worry about the destruction of society's foundations. "Homosexual marriage directly attacks the family, which is the most vital cell in society," argue Christian Coalition lawyers. "We must not allow this vital cell, the rock upon which society is built, to be inculturated with a perversion that will destroy it, and with it the future of our children and grandchildren. . . ." Cal Thomas, a nationally syndicated columnist, wrote, "Without a moral vision and the enforcement of morals at some level, cultures and then nations soon unravel. This is one of history's lessons for those who do not wish to repeat it."

Such things had not yet occurred as of 2010 in those states that permitted same-sex marriages or civil unions. In Vermont, no dire consequences were in evidence. Tourists had not disappeared, state government was not overburdened, and traditional families had suffered no discernible harm. A study in the Netherlands indicated that the institution of marriage was less transformed by including same-sex couples than gay identity was changed by the availability of marriage. On the basis of results such as these, supporters argue that same-sex marriage presents no threat to heterosexual marriage or to society in general. "From a conservative standpoint," said Theodore B. Olsen, former solicitor general under President George W. Bush, "people who wish to enter into the institution of marriage wish to enter into something that is the building block of our society, and that is itself a conservative value."

Opponents have argued that more divorces and fewer heterosexual marriages would follow in the wake of same-sex marriage. "It's impossible to be completely sure but it's hard to imagine how it would be otherwise," wrote David Blankenhorn, author of numerous articles on marriage. Yet preliminary data from Massachusetts indicates that after five years, the divorce rate in the state has dropped to historically low levels while the marriage rate has risen. Legal same-sex marriage is still relatively new, its opponents point out; its negative cultural results will take much longer to reveal themselves.

Some few conservatives make the pragmatic case that same-sex marriage will actually improve society by channeling homosexuals into long-term monogamous relationships and provide a more stable home for children. "Almost all the reasons to value opposite-sex marriage seem to me to apply to same-sex marriage," said law professor Eugene Volokh. "Marriage seems to on average make people happier. If it doesn't hurt others, and it helps the spouses, why not recognize it?"

Denigration of Marriage

Supporters argue that by wanting the right to marry, lesbians and gays reinforce the legitimacy of marriage. People usually wish to become part of an institution that they respect. Most Americans, gay or straight, view marriage as beneficial not only for the couple and their children but for society as a whole.

Yet this is not the view of same-sex marriage opponents. "The problem I have with same-sex marriage," said former New Mexico state senator Paul Becht, "is it denigrates the whole idea of marriage. Living together and having sex together is not the definition of marriage."

Accusing people of "denigrating" or "demeaning" marriage is bound to raise hackles, however honest the opinion. Take, for example, the following testy exchange in a 1996 debate in the House of Representatives over DOMA. The speakers were two prominent members of the House: Barney Frank of Massachusetts and Henry Hyde of Illinois.

> Hyde: People don't think the traditional marriage ought to be demeaned or trivialized by same-sex unions. If two men want to love each other, go right ahead. If you want to solemnize your love affair by some ceremony, create one. But don't take marriage, which for centuries has been a union between man and woman, and certainly is in this country, and try to say that what you're doing is American.
>
> Frank: I guess my problem is this. There are plenty of people here who have had marriages that have meant a great deal to them. I salute that. I don't for a minute understand how it demeans, and I would ask the gentleman to explain that to me. The gentleman's marriage, the marriages of other members here, are based on a deep love, a bond between two people. I don't think I demean it. I don't know how I could demean it. How does anything I do in which I express my feelings toward another demean the powerful bond of love and emotion and respect of two other people?

Congressman Barney Frank (D-MA) has been a vocal advocate of gay marriage. He has served in Congress for thirty years and has been openly gay since 1987. Frank lives with a domestic partner.

> Hyde: A loving relationship between people of the same sex ought to be their relationship. It ought to be private, and keep it private.
>
> Frank: You use the word "demean." How does it demean you?
>
> Hyde: Because many of us feel that there is an immoral—
>
> Frank: How does it demean your marriage? If other people are immoral, how does it demean your marriage? That's what you are saying.
>
> Hyde: It demeans the institution. It doesn't demean my marriage. My marriage was never demeaned. The institution of marriage is trivialized by same-sex marriage.

Same-sex-marriage supporters continue to argue that a desire to be joined in matrimony hardly undermines marriage or destroys the family. The future Pope Benedict XVI considered this very question in 2003: "It might be asked how a law can be contrary to the common good if it does not impose any particular kind of behavior, but simply gives legal recognition to a de facto reality which does not seem to cause injustice to anyone." He concluded that because laws exercise a wide influence, changes to them produce changes in the organization of society and harm the common good. "Legal recognition of homosexual unions," Cardinal Ratzinger said, "would mean not only the approval of deviant behavior . . . but would also obscure basic values which belong to the common inheritance of humanity."

It is difficult to determine the predictive value of these claims since they do not come with a time frame. How much time, one might ask, would have to elapse before same-sex marriage led to these detrimental changes? The LDS Church has stated that "it may be true that allowing single-sex unions will not immediately and directly affect all existing marriages." However, they add, "the real question is how it will affect society as a whole over time, including the rising generation and future generations." Because no one can predict the future with certainty, an argument that uses future hypotheticals is by its nature difficult to dispute.

Polygamy

Opponents of same-sex marriage often link it to the possibility of legalizing polygamy in the United States—a distinctly negative outcome in their eyes. Polygamy is a form of marriage in which a person has more than one spouse. If the right to marry is a fundamental right (as several courts have ruled) and denying same-sex couples the right to marry violates state constitutional guarantees of equality, then polygamists would seem to have the same rights to equal treatment under law.

Historically, polygamy is a form of social organization found in many cultures and at many times. Various sacred writings describe

Abraham, Jacob, David, Solomon, and Muhammad as all having had more than one wife. The practice still exists in parts of Africa as well as in Muslim countries. (Islam permits polygamy for men only, with a limit of four wives at any one time.)

In the United States, polygamy is most closely associated with the Church of Jesus Christ of Latter-day Saints. In the mid–1800s, LDS leader Brigham Young said that it was a religious duty for men to take multiple wives. But in 1890, the LDS Church publicly declared that, according to a new revelation, the church would

As is gay marriage, polygamy is illegal in the United States. Some supporters of marriage as the union between one man and one woman suggest that if gay marriage were legalized, it might open the door to polygamy.

no longer accept polygamous relationships. The "new revelation" paved the way for Utah's admission to the United States in 1896. The LDS Church remains opposed to polygamy and excommunicates any member who has more than one wife. However, several offshoots of the LDS Church, whose adherents are mostly found in rural parts of Utah, continue quietly to practice polygamy.

Polygamy is relevant to the same-sex marriage debate in two ways. First, it documents a rare but significant instance in which the U.S. Congress and Supreme Court (rather than the individual states) have regulated marriage. The Morrill Anti-Bigamy Act (1862) was the first in a series of federal laws designed to end the practice of polygamy. The LDS Church believed that the U.S. Constitution protected their religiously based practice of plural marriage. In 1878, George Reynolds told the U.S. Supreme Court that because he was a member of the LDS Church, polygamy was his religious duty, which he could violate only at the risk of eternal damnation. He claimed that laws against polygamy violated his right of freedom of religion under the First Amendment.

The U.S. Supreme Court disagreed. In *Reynolds* v. *United States*, a unanimous Supreme Court declared that polygamy was an offense against society and compared it to human sacrifice or the burning of women on their husbands' funeral pyres. The Court ruled, "Marriage, while from its very nature a sacred obligation, is nevertheless, in most civilized nations, a civil contract, and usually regulated by law . . . it is within the legitimate scope of the power of every civil government to determine whether polygamy or monogamy shall be the law of social life under its dominion."

Outside the LDS tradition, a majority of Americans have viewed polygamy negatively. "Polygamy has always been odious among the northern and western nations of Europe," asserted the Supreme Court in *Reynolds*. If legalizing same-sex marriage were to lead to legalizing polygamy and polygamy is so bad, then isn't that a reasonable ground on which to oppose same-sex marriage?

The Slippery Slope

A slippery-slope argument maintains that a given action, even a seemingly minor one, may be the first link in a chain of related actions, the inevitable result of which will be a significant impact of some sort. So with regard to same-sex marriage, former U.S. Senator Rick Santorum of Pennsylvania said, "If the Supreme Court says you have the right to consensual sex within your home, then you have the right to bigamy, you have the right to polygamy, you have the right to incest, you have the right to adultery. You have the right to anything."

Similarly, gay-marriage opponents argue that allowing same-sex couples to marry will logically lead to the fall of any and all legal restrictions on marriage. U.S. Supreme Court Justice Antonin Scalia adopted this position in his dissent in *Lawrence* v. *Texas*. Scalia wrote that if laws against homosexual conduct were unconstitutional, then state laws against polygamy, adult incest, prostitution, adultery, bestiality, and obscenity would also eventually be struck down.

Supporters respond in several ways. Many gay leaders distance their cause from polygamy; they are quick to dismiss analogies between polygamy and homosexuality. "Polygamy is a choice . . . homosexuality isn't," said one. "Polygamy is also terrible for society. It abuses women, creates a class of unmarried males (by leaving a shortage of single females) and leaves children unclear about their parents." They believe that same-sex marriages and polygamous marriages are sufficiently different for people and the legal system to recognize the fact. According to this view, every matter—whether polygamy, prostitution, or even incest—should be evaluated on its own merits.

Less common are same-sex-marriage supporters who see nothing wrong with the legalization (or at least decriminalization) of polygamy. They want the government completely out of the business of approving or disapproving religious matrimonial ceremonies. They believe that marital and sexual relations involving consenting adults should never be criminalized.

Slippery-slope arguments can lead to logical difficulties. "Slippery-slope diversions are what opponents of equality try when they don't have a good reason to justify ongoing discrimination," said one attorney. Such an argument ignores the possibility of any middle ground. Is it true that once an exception is made to some rule, nothing can hold back further and more extreme exceptions to that rule? One event might follow another, but the connection is not inevitable. Some specific linkage between events needs to be demonstrated.

Opponents believe they have found the logically consistent linkage between polygamy and same-sex marriage. It is founded on two theses: (1) If traditional marriage is the union of two people of different gender and (2) if the gender requirement is nothing but prejudice and an arbitrary denial of a person's choice in love, then the number restriction is a similarly arbitrary denial of individual choice.

Opponents point to the fact that polygamists could employ some of the same arguments used by gay rights supporters. For example, allowing people to enter into plural marriage would not prohibit others from marrying in the monogamous tradition. Churches would still be free to marry couples according to their own teachings. All people have a right to marry whomever they choose without outside interference. People who want to enter into polygamous marriages and those who want to enter into monogamous marriages should have equal rights. In a sense, polygamy supporters have a stronger case, because plural marriage has a long and established tradition in many parts of the world.

The passage of gay rights legislation seems to lend credence to the slippery-slope argument. Beginning in the 1960s, many states decriminalized homosexuality and later allowed same-sex couples to adopt. Some states banned discrimination against gay people in employment, housing, education, or public accommodations. When these changes were proposed, opponents warned that these laws were steps down a slippery slope to same-sex marriage. Gay rights supporters often dismissed these arguments as ridiculous.

For example, they assured people that a proposed antidiscrimination law in Massachusetts did not put the state on a slippery slope toward legalizing gay marriage.

Yet when the Massachusetts Supreme Judicial Court held that the state constitution required the legislature to recognize same-sex marriages, part of its reasoning rested on the legislature's decision to ban discrimination on the basis of sexual orientation. The Vermont Supreme Court used similar reasoning when it held that the state constitution required the legislature to recognize same-sex civil unions. It seems at least arguable that past liberalizations of traditional sexual rules led to further changes and that future liberalization will have similar effects.

Interracial Marriage

While some opponents of same-sex marriage point to polygamy as a reason for their stance, supporters have their own favorite historical analogy: the U.S. Supreme Court case aptly named *Loving* v. *Commonwealth of Virginia*.

In 1958, police officers arrested Richard and Mildred Loving in their Virginia bedroom and charged them with miscegenation (an interracial sexual relationship). The couple had been married in Washington, D.C., where interracial marriage was legal. At the time, Virginia was one of sixteen states that prohibited marriages based on race. As late as 1967, marriages involving a black person and a white person were against the law in all but one state south of the Mason-Dixon Line.

A Virginia court found the Lovings guilty of marrying out of state with intent to avoid Virginia's miscegenation law. The judge who sentenced them wrote in his decision, "Almighty God created the races white, black, yellow, Malay and red, and he placed them on separate continents. And but for the interference with his arrangement there would be no cause for such marriages. The fact that he separated the races shows that he did not intend for the races to mix."

Fifty years ago, Richard and Mildred Loving had to go to the Supreme Court in order to remain married—and out of jail! Richard Loving was white and Mildred black, and in Virginia in 1958, their union was illegal. Supporters of gay marriage point to the *Loving* case as a predecessor to their struggle.

That decision did not survive the civil rights era. In 1967, the U.S. Supreme Court ruled that the Virginia law was unconstitutional. In *Loving* v. *Commonwealth of Virginia*, the Supreme Court declared that the miscegenation law violated the equal-protection clause of the Constitution's Fourteenth Amendment. The nine justices unanimously ruled that race-based classifications were invidious (objectionable) by their very nature and permissible only if the government could show a specific compelling reason for writing them into the law.

In addition, the Court held that Virginia's miscegenation law violated the due-process clause because the right to marry "is one of the vital personal rights essential to the orderly pursuit of happiness by free men" and one that is "fundamental to our very existence and survival." The justices stated, "To deny this fundamental freedom on so unsupportable a basis as the racial classifications . . . is surely to deprive all the State's citizens of liberty without due process of law." The *Loving* case ended all race-based legal restrictions on marriage in the United States. Sociologists now estimate that about 7 percent of the United States's 59 million marriages involve mixed-race couples.

Certain aspects of the context of the case remain relevant to the same-sex-marriage debate. Gay rights supporters argue that civil rights issues should never be a question of popular will, since the problem with democracy is that the majority tends to oppress the minority. Interracial marriage was extremely unpopular in the 1950s and never would have passed if put to a vote of the people. A 1959 Gallup Poll showed that 96 percent of Americans disapproved of interracial marriage. As recently as 1998 in South Carolina and 2000 in Alabama, about 40 percent of the voters in each state voted to keep language barring interracial marriage in their respective state constitutions. One supporter of same-sex marriage argued, "Imagine the injury to our nation if the opposition (to racism) had prevailed with arguments like 'let the people vote' or with attacks on 'activist judges.'"

Some white southerners at the time used the slippery-slope argument and predicted that legal interracial marriage would lead to the fall of American society. Some Christians cited the Bible in opposition to interracial marriage. They called it an abomination for interracial couples to fall in love and predicted that it would destroy the institution of marriage. None of these things happened, and with a half-century's hindsight, the predictions look silly. Some apply this experience to same-sex marriage.

Does the *Loving* Decision Apply to Same-Sex Marriage?

Advocates claim that a ban on same-sex marriage is a form of sex discrimination, just as a ban on interracial marriage was a form of race discrimination. In *Loving*, lawyers for the state of Virginia argued that the state's law was permissible because it barred whites from marrying nonwhites just as much as it barred nonwhites from marrying whites. The Supreme Court completely rejected this "equal application" reasoning. The Court held that the law discriminated based on race because it determined eligibility to marry based on an individual's race.

The same logic may apply to laws against same-sex marriage. It would seem that a man is ineligible to marry another man solely because of his sex and a woman ineligible to marry a woman because of her sex. The fact that both sexes are forbidden from marrying same-sex partners does not eliminate this discrimination. In *Baehr* v. *Lewin*, the 1993 Hawaii Supreme Court relied on the precedent of *Loving* to question whether the ban on same-sex marriage was an unconstitutional sex-based classification.

Same-sex-marriage supporters have made the sex-discrimination argument in many other court cases but with mixed results. Many courts have refused to apply *Loving* to same-sex marriage. They read the law to say that racial classifications are uniquely invidious and less tolerable than gender-based classifications. In *Baker* v. *Vermont* (1999), the Vermont Supreme Court ruled that the state constitution required that equal benefits be extended to same-sex couples but rejected the analogy to *Loving* as "flawed." The court, while sympathetic to same-sex unions, stated that the plaintiffs "have not demonstrated that the exclusion of same-sex couples from the definition of marriage was intended to discriminate against women or lesbians and gay men, as racial segregation was designed to maintain the pernicious doctrine of white supremacy."

Other courts have found a different reason to restrict the *Loving* analogy. In *Andersen* v. *King County*, a 2006 Washington State case involving same-sex marriage, the Washington Supreme Court observed, "Whatever the history and tradition of interracial marriage had been, by the time *Loving* was decided, it had changed." In

1967, only sixteen states still banned interracial marriage, whereas forty-nine states prohibited same-sex marriage in 2006. The Washington court, believing this a matter of great importance, decided that there was no real history and tradition of same-sex marriage in the United States and that "the basic nature of marriage as a relationship between a man and a woman has not changed." The Massachusetts Supreme Judicial Court disagreed. In *Goodridge*, the SJC decided that the *Loving* decision did not depend on the "full-scale retreat" of miscegenation laws but instead turned on a "more fully developed understanding of the invidious quality of the discrimination."

In general, U.S. courts have preferred to read the *Loving* decision strictly in terms of race. In 2006, the New York Court of Appeals ruled in *Hernandez* v. *Robles* that the state constitution did not compel recognition of marriages between members of the same sex. The New York court specifically rejected any reliance upon the *Loving* case:

> [T]he historical background of *Loving* is different from the history underlying this case. Racism has been recognized for centuries—at first by a few people, and later by many more—as a revolting moral evil. . . . It is true that there has been serious injustice in the treatment of homosexuals also, a wrong that has been widely recognized only in the relatively recent past. . . . [But] the idea that same-sex marriage is even possible is a relatively new one. Until a few decades ago, it was an accepted truth for almost everyone who ever lived, in any society in which marriage existed, that there could be marriages only between participants of different sex. A court should not lightly conclude that everyone who held this belief was irrational, ignorant, or bigoted. We do not so conclude.

In 2007, gay rights supporters released a rare public statement from Mildred Loving in support of same-sex marriage on the fortieth anniversary of the *Loving* v. *Commonwealth of Virginia* decision. She concluded, "I believe all Americans, no matter their race, no matter their sex, no matter their sexual orientation, should have that same freedom to marry. Government has no business imposing some people's religious beliefs over others. Especially if it denies people's civil rights." After her death, the Loving family supposedly denied that she held these views.

Is Same-Sex Marriage a Civil Rights Issue?

In the *Loving* decision, the Supreme Court included language about the fundamental importance of the right to marry. Is same-sex marriage also a civil rights issue?

One Massachusetts state representative denied that gay people were in any way oppressed or denied their civil rights. He supported a constitutional amendment to ban same-sex marriage by asking rhetorically, "Are gay people denied the right to vote? Are they denied employment? Are they denied home ownership?" Same-sex-marriage supporters disagree. They believe that they are not fighting for preferential treatment but instead trying to right a common and socially harmful form of discrimination. "Gay rights, after all, are nothing more than non-gay rights made available to all," said one supporter.

Same-sex-marriage supporters have tried to paint same-sex marriage as a "marriage-equality movement" and link it to the civil rights battles of the 1950s and 1960s. African-American civil rights icons, including Coretta Scott King, Julian Bond, and John Lewis, have played a role in supporting same-sex marriage. Some advocates even dislike using the term "same-sex marriage" or "gay marriage" because these terms imply that same-sex couples are asking for rights and privileges that married couples do not have. Said one supporter, "We

Hundreds of thousands marched on Washington, D.C., in 2009 for the National Equality March.

don't want 'gay marriage,' we want marriage—the same freedom to marry, with the same duties, dignity, security, and expression of love and equality as our non-gay brothers and sisters have."

However, opponents deny there is anything called a "right to marry." A person cannot marry more than one partner at a time or marry an immediate member of one's family. One opponent ridiculed same-sex marriage as a right that never occurred to anyone until "the day before yesterday." The LDS Church stated, "It is not the purpose of government to provide legal protection to every possible way in which individuals may pursue fulfillment."

Moreover, many African Americans believe gay people and their allies "are trying to hijack the moral capital of the black civil rights movement and use it to affirm their behavior, regardless of other people's moral beliefs about it." Walter Fauntroy, a noted African-American civil rights leader, conceded that the struggles of black people and gay people for rights are exactly the same when it comes to access to income, education, health care, housing, and criminal justice. Yet he supported a constitutional amendment defining marriage as the union of a man and a woman because "my religious tradition says (homosexuality) is an abomination."

Many African-American religious leaders describe gay identity as a lifestyle choice and see no parallel to race-based discrimination, because race is not a choice. One African-American clergyman said, "For them to compare the civil rights with gay rights—it should be offensive to every African American in the whole United States." Another said, "As an African American, I find it highly offensive to associate homosexuality with civil rights . . . race and sexuality have nothing to do with each other." A Chicago minister voiced an extreme form of this position: "If the K.K.K. opposes gay marriage, I would ride with them." Yet that position is far from unanimous. In the debate over same-sex marriage in the District of Columbia in 2009 and 2010, local African-American ministers were to be found on both sides of the question.

Activist Judges

One of the complaints of opponents of same-sex marriage is that activist judges in the states of California, Connecticut, Vermont, and Iowa have overstepped the constitutional authority of the judicial branch. They believe that controversial issues such as same-sex marriage should be left to a vote of the people, either through their elected representatives in the legislature or by ballot-initiatives. "CALIFORNIANS HAVE NEVER VOTED FOR SAME-SEX MARRIAGE," trumpeted one brochure favoring Proposition 8. "If gay activists want to legalize gay marriage, they should put it on the ballot. Instead, they have gone behind the backs of the voters and convinced four activist judges in San Francisco to redefine marriage for the rest of society."

Even some judges have taken this position. One Massachusetts judge dissented in the *Goodridge* case, saying, "[W]hat is at stake in this case . . . is the power of the Legislature to effectuate social change without interference from the courts." He emphasized that the "power to regulate marriage lies with the legislature, not with the judiciary."

A similar argument was made in California in the *In re Marriage Cases*. The dissenting judges claimed the majority had violated the separation of powers by giving itself the power to make a significant legislative policy judgment without any clear constitutional directive. The dissenting justices stated, "If there is to be a further sea change in the social and legal understanding of marriage itself, that evolution should occur by similar democratic means. The majority forecloses this ordinary democratic process, and, in doing so, oversteps its authority."

As of 2010, when the people have voted, they have rejected same-sex marriage in almost every case. In 2006, Arizona became the only state ever to defeat a constitutional amendment defining marriage as necessarily involving a man and a woman, but a similar amendment passed two years later. Such electoral results carry great weight with many Americans. "As a self-governing nation, the power should ultimately rest with 'we the people,'" wrote one opponent of same-sex marriage. "We have seen before how judicial activists that see themselves as God's tool for the cultural and legal 'advancement' of society can take the law in their own hands and even circumvent the will of the people in order to bring what they see as "progress."

Same-sex-marriage supporters argue that the vote of the people is not quite as decisive as it seems. In some cases, the votes have been one-sided—86 percent in Mississippi and 81 percent in Alabama and Tennessee. In other cases, the vote has been much closer—52 percent in California and 53 percent in Maine and Washington. Millions of people have voted to support same-sex marriage and have done so in far larger percentages than ever supported interracial marriage. According to some polls, popular support approaches a majority in several states. Were those states to vote their approval, would opponents be willing to recognize then that "the people have spoken"? Or is the argument used only because same-sex marriage has gone down to defeat every time?

Other supporters contend that the vote of the people is irrelevant because questions regarding equal treatment under the law and due process require a response from the court. Since the American system of checks and balances leaves it to the judiciary branch to protect the basic rights of minority groups against the tyranny of the majority, supporters believe that judges should strike down gender-restrictive marriage laws in the same way that they struck down racially restrictive marriage laws.

In *Baker* v. *Vermont* (1999), the Vermont court anticipated the accusation that "the small group of men and women comprising this Court has no business deciding an issue of such enormous moment." They tried to explain the reasoning for their ruling:

> This case came before us because citizens of the state invoked their constitutional right to seek redress through the judicial process of a perceived deprivation under

state law. The Vermont Constitution does not permit the courts to decline to adjudicate a matter because its subject is controversial, or because the outcome may be deeply offensive to the strongly held beliefs of many of our citizens. . . . To the contrary, if a case has been brought before us, and if the established procedures have been followed, as they were here, we must hear and decide it. Moreover, we must decide the case on legal grounds. However much history, sociology, religious belief, personal experience, or other considerations may inform our individual or collective deliberations, we must decide this case, and all cases, on the basis of our understanding of the law, and the law alone.

This rationale has not assuaged everyone's anger. "[T]he fact is that the enemies of marriage will never cease to attack traditional marriage until society, not only accepts their relationships, but in fact promotes them as good and desirable," wrote a California lawyer. "To them, constitutions, laws, and votes do not matter. Blinded by their ambition, they will trample on anything or anyone to obtain what they want. . . . Proponents of same-sex 'marriage' seek to overturn the will of the people. . . ."

6 The Future of Same-Sex Marriage

ANY PREDICTION ON THE FUTURE OF SAME-SEX marriage in the United States or elsewhere in the world would appear to be no more than a wild guess. Political and social systems can sometimes go unchanged for a long time, only to reach a tipping point where rapid change occurs. At the same time, constitutional amendments against same-sex marriage in most states may imply a long period of defeat for gay and lesbian causes. It is impossible to tell if the American backlash against same-sex marriage will endure in the short or long term.

In the United States, polls seem to imply that while support for same-sex marriage is building, voters resist when they feel the issue is being pushed too rapidly. A national poll in 2009 found that 33 percent of respondents said that gay couples should be allowed to marry legally, 30 percent said they should not be allowed to marry but should be allowed to enter into civil unions, and 32 percent said they should have no legal recognition. A plurality of Americans expect gay marriage to be legal in their lifetime, and that belief is much stronger among the young. Almost every poll shows that younger Americans, regardless of where they live or of their religion, support same-sex marriage. "The reality is that the judicial decisions were substantially ahead of public opinion, and still are," said one gay rights supporter. "The center of gravity is

In March 2009, demonstrators for and against gay marriage rallied in front of the California Supreme Court Building, where arguments were heard for and against Proposition 8. This prohibition against gay marriage was upheld in 2010.

clearly moving, but at the moment, marriage is a bridge too far for many voters."

A good indicator of the state of American popular opinion is to be found in the referendums on same-sex marriage in California and Maine. Based on those two votes (2008 and 2009, respectively), Rubén Díaz Sr., a member of the New York State Senate, said, "The people of the nation don't want gay marriage. They didn't want it in California; they didn't want it in Maine. . . . Forget about it. People don't want it." Since both elections were close, Díaz may be overstating the case. About half of Maine's eligible voters went to the polls, and they voted to reject same-sex marriage by a margin of 53 to 47 percent. In California, 79 percent of eligible voters turned out on Election Day, 52 percent of whom agreed that only marriage between a man and a woman should be valid in California.

It is indisputable that American attitudes regarding homosexuality have softened since 1990. As recently as 1993, nearly half of all respondents in a national poll indicated they were disgusted by the thought of homosexuality, and more than a third were strongly disgusted. Since then, hostility toward same-sex activity has lessened markedly. Whether this trend will continue, level off, or reverse is unknown.

Despite the change in attitude toward homosexuality, most Americans' views of the nature of marriage are little changed. Many say they are uncomfortable with the thought of gays and lesbians marrying. A majority believe that gay marriage violates their religious beliefs, and nearly half of those polled say that if their church performed same-sex marriages, they would find another church. Same-sex marriage is not about to sweep the nation as long as it is a matter of state-by-state popular vote.

Voters in Maine in 2009 voted against the legalization of gay marriage.

Federalism and the Future of DOMA

In the United States, the principle of decentralized power is the foundation of American federalism. Thus, each state has its own laws governing civil marriage. Each is free to set the conditions for a valid marriage, subject only to the limits set by the state and U.S. constitutions. States differ on the minimum marriageable age and on whether first cousins can marry.

At the same time, marital status has been "portable"; the validity of a couple's marriage is recognized from state to state and even country to country. A couple married in Hawaii could feel confident that Alaska and Florida would not question their status. Because the federal Defense of Marriage Act (DOMA) provides that no state has to recognize a same-sex marriage effected in another state, many of the act's opponents say that it violates the full-faith-and-credit clause of the Constitution.

Law professors are divided on DOMA's constitutionality. Supporters and opponents both recognize that noteworthy historical exceptions to the full-faith-and-credit clause exist. Courts have allowed states to refuse to recognize a marriage if the marriage violates a "strong public policy" of the state, even if the marriage was legal in the state where it was performed. States historically have used this public-policy exception to refuse to recognize out-of-state polygamous marriages, underage marriages, incestuous marriages, and interracial marriages. Opponents of gay marriage argue that the public-policy-exception precedent allows states to refuse recognition to same-sex marriages even without DOMA. They claim that all that is necessary is that a state pass a law or amend its own constitution to declare such unions impermissible.

President Barack Obama's political platform in 2008 included the promise of the full repeal of DOMA. He said that he believed states should have the right to determine the question of marriage. Yet in June 2009, the Department of Justice stunned gay rights supporters by issuing a brief defending the constitutionality of DOMA in the case of *Smelt* v. *United States of America*. In February 2011, the Obama administration announced that it would no longer enforce DOMA. Still, a 2009 congressional bill to repeal DOMA appeared unlikely to pass. Although several lawsuits attacking DOMA's constitutionality were making their way through the courts, the U.S. Supreme Court had not yet accepted one for review.

In law, the concept of comity refers to the idea that one jurisdiction will extend certain courtesies to other jurisdictions. In the United States, the term is usually applied to legal relations between the states—the voluntary decision by the courts of one state to accept the decision of another state on a similar issue.

Yet, as states come to different conclusions regarding same-sex marriage, the problem of comity intensifies. Many states have been reluctant to recognize other states' same-sex marriages. This problem is compounded by the fact that, as with traditional marriages, all same-sex marriages do not last until death. As a result, state courts are beginning to deal with divorce and child-custody cases involving same-sex couples. State legislatures and courts have sent mixed messages about whether same-sex couples can divorce in a state that does not allow legal same-sex marriage. For example, Indiana and Rhode Island have both denied divorces to gay couples who were married elsewhere. Yet in a similar case, New Jersey granted a divorce.

Many supporters believe that after a period of initial resistance, comity for gay marriage will inevitably follow. They believe that everyone involved in legal and custody cases will decide that maintaining a gay-marriage exception to comity complicates matters too much. Some recent legal cases seem to lean that way. In 2007, a federal appeals court examined Oklahoma's refusal to recognize final adoption orders of other states that permitted adoption by same-sex couples (Oklahoma does not allow same-sex couples to adopt). In *Finstuen* v. *Crutcher* (2007), the court ruled that Oklahoma's adoption law was unconstitutional. It is not clear whether same-sex marriage is a similar type of case.

It is perfectly possible to have a system where some states recognize same-sex marriages and other states do not. The system may not create overwhelming legal or public policy problems; after all, there is no uniform national family law or national criminal code. The states' differing family-law policies, including their differing requirements for marriage, have not created impossible levels of confusion.

Around the World

In countries around the globe, the institution of marriage is in flux. Lawmakers are considering whether to allow gay and lesbian couples the right to marry or enter into other recognized forms of domestic partnership. As of 2011, some countries, mostly in Europe, were offering varying levels of marriage rights to same-sex couples.

In 2001, the Netherlands became the first country to authorize same-sex marriage. It is also recognized in Canada, Belgium, Norway, Sweden, Iceland, and South Africa. In 2010, Portugal and Spain, countries with large Catholic populations, legalized same-sex marriage despite the formal opposition of the Catholic Church.

Some countries that have not legalized gay marriage have revised their laws to reflect changed social situations. Uruguay, Colombia, Ecuador, New Zealand, and most European nations now allow some form of civil union, a legal status that gives gay couples rights similar to those of married couples concerning property, inheritance, pension, immigration, tax benefits, and other legal matters.

Yet as of 2010, Ireland and Italy did not allow same-sex unions. Poland's and Latvia's constitutions were amended to define marriage in such a way as to ban same-sex marriage.

Countries in Latin America, a region with a large Catholic population, have also paid more attention to same-sex marriage and gay rights. In 2009, Uruguay became the first Latin American country to allow same-sex adoption. Uruguay, Colombia, and Ecuador have recognized civil unions for same-sex couples.

In July 2010, when its senate approved (33–27) a law authorizing same-sex marriages, Argentina became the first country in Latin America to allow gay couples to wed. Buenos Aires, a famously gay-friendly city, first allowed same-sex civil unions in 2002. One gay Argentinean said, "we have the right to the same legal status in the eyes of the law and deserve to be given the same legal protection as heterosexual couples." Catholic opponents warned that same-sex marriage could speed the decline of traditional values in South

Federal Marriage Amendment

Some of the firmest opponents of same-sex marriage want to amend the U.S. Constitution to prohibit it. The Federal Marriage Amendment (FMA), also called the Marriage Protection Amendment (by supporters), would limit the definition of marriage in the United States to the union of one man and one woman. The FMA would also prevent judges from extending marriage rights to same-sex couples and polygamists. It has been proposed several times with slightly different wording.

That it is not easy to amend the U.S. Constitution may be seen from the fact that over the course of more than two centuries, only twenty-seven amendments have been ratified. An amendment requires the support of a two-thirds majority in each house of Congress and then ratification by three-fourths of the states (thirty-eight states). The FMA was introduced in the U.S. Congress four times between 2003 and 2008. In a vote in the House of Representatives in 2006, the FMA attained a 236–187 margin of approval, but it fell far short of the 290 yes votes needed to pass. The Senate has never voted directly on the amendment.

Advocates of the FMA argue that it is necessary to protect marriage from activist judges. Opponents claim that the FMA would violate principles of federalism; they believe that the federal government has no reason to intervene in what has primarily been a state issue.

A similar attempt to take the issue of same-sex marriage out of the hands of the states was the so-called Marriage Protection Act (MPA) of 2007. This was a proposed law, not a constitutional amendment. The MPA's purpose was to change the federal law code to deny federal courts the right to decide any question relating to the interpretation of the Defense of Marriage Act (DOMA) or the MPA itself. This type of law is known as "jurisdiction stripping": it strips local or state courts of their right to make a decision or even hear a case.

Like DOMA, the Marriage Protection Act raises constitutional questions in relation to the full-faith-and-credit clause. In 2004, the bill passed the House of Representatives but failed in the Senate. Both the Marriage Protection Act and the Federal Marriage Amendment appeared to have considerable support but not enough to pass as of 2010.

America. Jorge Bergoglio, the archbishop of Buenos Aires, called the new law "a destructive attack on God's plan."

In December 2009, the local assembly of Mexico City voted to make it the first Latin American city to legalize same-sex marriage by redefining marriage as "the free uniting of two people." It also guaranteed gay and lesbian couples the right to adopt children, apply for joint loans, and inherit a spouse's wealth. Almost 300 weddings had taken place as of July 2010. Mexico's government has challenged the city's action in the nation's supreme court.

In December 2009, Mexico City became the first Latin American city to legalize gay marriage.

The liberalizing trend is not universal. The constitution of Bolivia in 2008 banned same-sex marriage and restricted civil unions to opposite-sex couples. Honduras barred gay couples from marrying or adopting children in 2005.

In Africa, homosexuality is widely seen as an immoral European import; the laws of many African countries deal with it severely. In northern Nigeria, gay men can face death by stoning. In Sierra Leone, a lesbian activist was raped and stabbed to death at her desk in 2004. Zimbabwean president Robert Mugabe dismissed gays as "lower than pigs and dogs." In Uganda in 2009, a proposed bill imposed the death sentence for homosexual behavior. James Nsaba Buturo, Uganda's minister of ethics and integrity, said simply, "Homosexuals can forget about human rights." In many African countries, a conviction for homosexual acts may bring more jail time than rape or murder. Only in South Africa is homosexuality widely accepted and protected by law.

The Fall of Civil Unions?

When Vermont initiated the concept of civil unions in 1999, the idea appeared to be an appealing compromise in the same-sex-marriage debate. Yet only ten years later, the civil-union solution seems to have failed. Study commissions in Vermont and New Jersey concluded that the new status did not operate well, either from misunderstanding or from outright hostility. Couples trying to exercise rights included in civil-union status—such as access to spousal insurance benefits and hospital-visitation privileges—were often denied them, even in their home states. They experienced even greater difficulties when traveling or moving out of state, especially to a state that did not have or recognize their status. The California Supreme Court, in the *In re Marriage Cases* decision (2008), noted at least nine specific differences between marriages and civil unions in state law.

In 2007, the Vermont commission declared that "civil unions are separate, but unequal" and supported extending full marriage rights to same-sex couples. "[P]roviding statutory access to marriage would be a clearer and more direct statement of full equality by the state," the commission suggested. It would also be "a statement of full inclusion of its gay and lesbian residents in the bundle of rights, obligations, protections, and responsibilities flowing from the status of civil marriage." The Vermont legislature authorized same-sex couples to marry in the state beginning on September 1, 2009.

In 2008, the Connecticut Supreme Court ruled in *Kerrigan* v. *Commissioner of Public Health* that failing to give same-sex couples the full rights, responsibilities, and name of marriage violated the

Same-sex marriage map

● Country where homosexual marriage is legal *(chronological order, 2001 - 2010)*

● States where it is authorized

● Countries where a "civil union" between homosexuals is permitted

Though many countries throughout the world do not allow gay marriage, some now do. This map shows the distribution of same-sex unions and gay marriage rights worldwide.

state constitution's equal-protection clause. The court's majority opinion stated that civil unions could not serve as an acceptable substitute: "Although marriage and civil unions do embody the same legal rights under our law, they are by no means 'equal.' . . . The former is an institution of transcendent historical, cultural, and social significance, whereas the latter most surely is not." In 2009, lawmakers of Connecticut overwhelmingly repealed the old marriage laws and rewrote all references to marriage in gender-neutral terms. As of 2010, Connecticut no longer provided civil unions and converted all existing civil unions automatically to marriages. New Hampshire's legislature made a similar decision; as of 2011, all civil unions in the state automatically became marriages.

Opponents are unhappy with this turn of events. A Connecticut official argued that it was far too early—after only three years—to say that civil unions signified second-class status. "Our experience with civil unions is simply too new," complained one opponent, "and the views of the people of our state about it as a social institution are too much in flux to say with any certitude that the marriage statute must be struck down in order to vindicate the plaintiffs' constitutional rights."

Nonetheless, Vermont's experience between 1999 and 2009 may turn out to serve as a blueprint for same-sex marriage nationwide. In 1999, the Vermont legislature accepted civil unions only reluctantly. Yet a decade later, they granted full marriage rights to gay couples without any pressure from the courts. The national timeline may be more protracted, but it may happen that full marriage rights will follow the passage of civil unions in states.

The Situation by 2011

Between 2003 and 2010, seven U.S. states and the District of Columbia legalized same-sex marriage. In two of the seven—California (2008) and Maine (2009)—statewide referendums restricted marriage to straight couples. Therefore, by 2011, same-sex marriage was legal in five states—New Hampshire, Massachusetts, Vermont, Iowa, and Connecticut—and the District of Columbia. New York, Rhode Island, and New Mexico did not permit same-sex marriages but recognized such marriages performed elsewhere. Several other states, including California, New Jersey, Washington, Hawaii, Maine, Maryland, Colorado, Wisconsin, Nevada, and Oregon, allowed same-sex couples to enter into civil unions or domestic partnerships. By the same time, thirty-one states had passed state constitutional amendments by popular vote defining marriage as the union of one man and one woman.

On August 4, 2010, the fate of California's Proposition 8 was temporarily decided in a federal San Francisco courtroom: the proposition was struck down by the judge, but his decision was immediately stayed (that is, not put into effect) pending an appeal to the Ninth Circuit Court of Appeals. In *Perry* v. *Schwarzenegger*, two gay couples had argued that Proposition 8 violated the Constitution's guarantees of equal protection and due process. Their lawyers had made the familiar claims that the right to marry was a fundamental right and that the government had no rational basis to restrict marriage to opposite-sex couples. In response, the leading sponsor of Proposition 8 had argued that "to invalidate the people's vote, the plaintiffs have . . . to prove the people acted irrationally. That does not mean that there has to be choice between whether gay marriage is good or gay marriage is bad, but do the people have a right to decide?"

Opponents of same-sex marriage have continued to assert that the issue should be decided by popular vote or through the legislative process rather than by the judiciary. Gay rights advocates feel that no legislative action or popular majority can deny a minority a fundamental civil right. These positions are irreconcilable and will remain so unless a majority of the American people come to support same-sex marriage. Such a turnabout seems unlikely in the short term.

The language of the controversy has grown strident. Yet even amid the harsh words, there are signs that outside the courts people still get along with one another. The case of one New York state senator from the Bronx is illustrative. Rubén Díaz Sr. is one of the chief opponents of same-sex marriage in the New York State Senate, yet two of his brothers and a granddaughter are gay. Díaz's personal attorney is also gay; he lives with his partner in Queens. Díaz and his wife often double-date with them. "I love them. I love them. But I don't believe in what they are doing," he said. "They are my brothers. They are my family. So how could I be a homophobe. . . . My religion is against gay marriage. It means, I don't agree with what you do. But let's go out. Let's go to the movies. Let's be friends."

Most gay men and lesbians agree that over the last forty years they have made enormous strides in terms of increased public acceptance and civil rights. However, there is a gap between their social acceptance and society's *legal* acceptance of same-sex marriage. In the United States that gap has narrowed in the twenty-first century. Whether it will ever close completely remains a matter of controversy.

Notes

Chapter 1

p. 5, "[T]he right to marry . . . ": "In the Supreme Court of California, *In re Marriage Cases*," May 15, 2008, caselaw.lp.findlaw.com/data2/californiastatecases/s147999.pdf

p. 6, *Varnum* v. *Brien*," Supreme Court of Iowa, April 3, 2009, caselaw.lp.findlaw.com/data2/californiastatecases/s147999.pdf

p. 6, "Every successful social movement . . . ": Laura Listwood in Craig Rimmerman and Clyde Wilcox, eds., *The Politics of Same-Sex Marriage* (Chicago: University of Chicago Press, 2007), p. 241.

p. 6, "Advocates for same-sex marriage . . . ": Jeremy Peters, "New York Senate Turns Back Bill on Gay Marriage," *New York Times*, December 3, 2009.

p. 10, "institution of marriage . . .": *Baker* v. *Nelson*, Supreme Court of Minnesota, 1971, http://www.cas.umt.edu/phil/faculty/Walton/bakrvnel.htm

p. 10, "for want of a substantial . . .": Marcia Coyle, "California Case May Turn on 1972 Ruling," *National Law Journal*, August 23, 2010, http://www.law.com/jsp/nlj/PubArticleNLJ.jsp?id=1202470861873&slreturn=1&hbxlogin=1

p. 14, "who seek nothing more or less . . .": Jeffrey Amestoy, "Uncommon Humanity: Reflections on Judging in a Post-Human Era," *New York University Law Review* 78 (November 2003), pp. 1581–1595, http://www1.law.nyu.edu/journals/lawreview/issues/vol78/no5/index.html

p. 14, "Supporters and opponents alike . . . ": Elizabeth Mehren, "Vermont Senate OKs 'Marriage' Rights for Gays," *Los Angeles Times*, April 20, 2000, http://articles.latimes.com/2000/apr/20/news/mn-21588

p. 15, "The present case . . .": *Lawrence* v. *Texas*, Findlaw, 2003, http://caselaw.lp.findlaw.com/scripts/getcase.pl?court=us&vol=000&invol=02-102

p. 15, "They argued that the majority had . . . ": Michael Mello, *Legalizing Gay Marriage* (Philadelphia: Temple University Press, 2004).

pp. 15–16, "Deny the protections . . .": *Goodridge* v. *Department of Public Health*, Findlaw, 2003, news.findlaw.com/wp/docs/conlaw/goodridge 111803opn.pdf

p. 16, "Over the next year . . . ": "*Goodridge* v. *Department of Public Health*," Findlaw, November 18, 2003, www.google.com/search?hl=en &source=hp&ie=ISO-8859-1&q=findlaw+goodridge

p. 17, "Let's be clear . . . ": Pinello, pp. 18–19; Michael Mello, *Legalizing Gay Marriage* (Philadelphia: Temple University Press, 2004), pp. 7–11.

p. 17, "[O]ur rights as Americans . . . " John Lewis, "At a Crossroads on Gay Unions," *Boston Globe*, October 25, 2003, www.boston.com/news/globe/ editorial_opinion/oped/articles/2003/10/25/at_a_crossroads_on_gay_ unions/

Chapter 2

p. 19, "the family as it has been known . . .": James Dobson, *Focus on the Family Newsletter*, April 2004.

p. 20, "Civil marriage . . . ": "*Goodridge* v. *Department of Public Health*," Findlaw, November 18, 2003, www.google.com/search?hl=en &source=hp&ie=ISO-8859-1&q=findlaw+goodridge

p. 20, "If two complete . . . ": Evan Wolfson, *Why Marriage Matters: America, Equality, and Gay People's Right to Marry* (New York: Simon and Schuster, 2004), p. 10.

p. 22, "We expose . . . ": Michael Mello, *Legalizing Gay Marriage* (Philadelphia: Temple University Press, 2004), p. 28.

p. 23, "Marriage is not . . . ": Robert Baird and Stuart Rosenbaum, eds., *Same-Sex Marriage: The Moral and Legal Debate* (Amherst, NY: Prometheus Books, 1997), pp. 164–168.

p. 23, "As late as 1994 . . . ": Poll cited in Craig Rimmerman and Clyde Wilcox, eds., *The Politics of Same-Sex Marriage* (Chicago: University of Chicago Press, 2007), pp. 215–242.

p. 23, "We're frustrated by the suggestion . . . ": Sarah Wildman, "Children Speak for Same-Sex Marriage," *New York Times*, January 21, 2010.

p. 23, "If we are seeing . . . ": Sarah Wildman, "Children Speak for Same-Sex Marriage," *New York Times*, January 21, 2010.

p. 23, "Gay people should have …": Roy Rivenburg, "Divided over Gay

Marriage," *Los Angeles Times*, March 12, 2004, http://articles.latimes.com/2004/mar/12/entertainment/et-rivenburg12

p. 24, "Almost no one . . . ": Evan Wolfson, *Why Marriage Matters: America, Equality, and Gay People's Right to Marry* (New York: Simon and Schuster, 2004), p. 130.

pp. 24–25, "Anything less than marriage . . . ": Michael Mello, *Legalizing Gay Marriage* (Philadelphia: Temple University Press, 2004), pp. 142–192.

p. 25, "Some say let's choose . . . ": John Lewis, "At a Crossroads on Gay Unions," *Boston Globe*, October 25, 2003, www.boston.com/news/globe/editorial_opinion/oped/articles/2003/10/25/at_a_crossroads_on_gay_unions/

p. 31, "Yet Boswell . . . ": John Boswell, *Same-Sex Unions in Premodern Europe* (New York: Random House, 1994), pp. 162–218.

p. 32, "they married one another . . .": Andrew Sullivan, *Same-Sex Marriage, Pro and Con* (New York: Vintage, Rev. Ed. 2004).

p. 34, "Sodomy is so filthy . . . ": R. Moore, *The Formation of a Persecuting Society: Power and Deviance in Western Europe, 950–1250* (Malden, MA: Blackwell, 1987), p. 93.

p. 39, "unlikely that a few thousand . . . ": Roy Rivenburg, "Divided over Gay Marriage," *Los Angeles Times*, March 12, 2004, http://articles.latimes.com/2004/mar/12/entertainment/et-rivenburg12

p. 39, "until such time . . . ": "*Goodridge* v. *Department of Public Health*." Findlaw, November 18, 2003, http://fl1.findlaw.com/news.findlaw.com/wp/docs/conlaw/goodridge111803opn.pdf

p. 39, "The biggest challenge . . . ": Jesse McKinley, "Fight to Reverse California's Same-Sex Marriage Ban Heads to Courtroom," *New York Times*, January 11, 2010.

Chapter 3

p. 41, "Homosexuality intimacy . . . ": Duke Helfand, "Doctrine Disputes Grow As Gays Wed," *Los Angeles Times*, June 19, 2008, http://articles.latimes.com/2008/jun/19/local/me-scripture19.

pp. 41–42, "Those who favor . . . ": "The Divine Institution of Marriage," LDS Newsroom, August 13, 2008, http://newsroom.lds.org/ldsnewsroom/eng/commentary/the-divine-institution-of-marriage

p. 42, "We respect the right . . . " Evan Wolfson, *Why Marriage Matters: America, Equality, and Gay People's Right to Marry* (New York: Simon and Schuster, 2004), p. 109.

p. 42, "In *Baehr* v. *Lewin* . . . ": "*Baehr* v. *Lewin.*" Hawaii Supreme Court, May 5, 1993, www.danpinello.com/Baehr.htm

p. 44, "It is impossible for Judaism ..." Andrew Sullivan, ed., *Same-Sex Marriage: Pro and Con* (New York: Vintage, 1997), pp. 61–66.

p. 45, "I do not believe that God . . . ": Sharon Kleinbaum and Margaret Wenig, *There's a Place for Us: Gays and Lesbians in the Jewish Community* (Woodstock, VT: Jewish Lights, 2002), p. 5.

p. 45, "Discarding the historical definition . . . ": "Aguda, O.U. Oppose N.Y. Same-Sex Marriage Bill." *JTA*, May 8, 2009, http://jta.org/news/article/2009/05/08/1005028/agudath-ou-oppose-ny-same-sex-marriage-bill

p. 48, "The Roman Catholic . . . ": Andrew Sullivan, ed., *Same-Sex Marriage: Pro and Con* (New York: Vintage, 1997), pp. 52–53.

p. 48, "Where homosexual unions . . . ": Joseph Ratzinger, "Considerations Regarding Proposals to Give Legal Recognition to Unions between Homosexual Persons," July 2003. www.vatican.va/roman_curia/congregations/cfaith/documents/rc_con_cfaith_doc_20030731_homosexual-unions_en.html

p. 49, "Oppose steadfastly . . . ": Southern Baptist Convention, "On Same-Sex Marriage, Resolutions," June 2003, www.sbc.net/resolutions/amResolution.asp?ID=1128.

p. 49, "The church, with about a million . . . ": United Church of Christ, Resolutions, "Equal Marriage Rights for All," July 4, 2005, http://pewforum.org/docs/?DocID=291

p. 50, "Yet the Lutheran Church . . . " "Swedish Lutherans Allow Gay Marriage," *Euronews*, October 22, 2009, www.euronews.net/2009/10/22/swedish-lutherians-allow-gay-marriage/

p. 50, "unscriptural, unnatural, and totally . . .": http://www.modernghana.com/news/43960/1/west-african-province-of-anglican-church-breaks-aw.html

p. 50, "the total rejection of . . .": http://www.anglican-nig.org/PH2006message2nation.htm

pp. 52–53, "same-sex marriage is out . . . ": Onwuka Nzeshi, "Nigeria: Homosexuals Kick against Same-Sex Prohibition Bill," Allafrica.com, March 12, 2009, http://allafrica.com/stories/200903120085.html

p. 53, "support of gay and lesbian . . .": http://www.episcopalarchives.org/cgi-bin/acts/acts_search.pl

p. 54, "a violation of God's law . . .": http://www.shuracouncil.org/

images/special/2008Advisories/52208Advisory.htm

p. 54, "The Church's teachings . . . ": Jennifer Dobner, "Film Focuses on Mormon Role in Gay Marriage Ban," AP, January 23, 2010, http://abcnews.go.com/Entertainment/wireStory?id=9643209

p. 54, "one of the great moral . . . " Church of Jesus Christ of Latter-day Saints, "The Divine Institution of Marriage," LDS Newsroom, August 13, 2008, http://newsroom.lds.org/ldsnewsroom/eng/commentary/the-divine-institution-of-marriage

p. 55. "The people in California . . . " Jen Chaney, "'8: The Mormon Proposition': Audacious Look at Church's Role in Gay-Marriage Ban," *Washington Post*, January 30, 2010, www.washingtonpost.com/wpdyn/content/article/2010/01/29/AR2010012904041.html

p. 55, "speaking out . . . " Church of Jesus Christ of Latter-day Saints, "The Divine Institution of Marriage."

p. 55, "the greatest threat . . . ": Aaron Falk, "Gays Greatest Threat to America, Buttars Says," *Deseret News* (Salt Lake City), February 19, 2009, www.deseretnews.com/article/1,5143,705285940,00.html

pp. 55–56, "Gay marriages do not . . . ": Ruth Vanita, *Love's Rite: Same-Sex Marriage in India and the West* (New Delhi: Penguin Books India, 2005), p. 308.

p. 56, "marriage is a union . . . ": Vanita, pp. 307–309.

p. 56, "against the Sikh religion . . . ": http://www.cbc.ca/news/canada/story/2005/03/28/sikhguy-050328.html

p. 56, "One Sikh legislator in Canada . . . ": Kevin Bourassa and Joe Varnell, "Purging Toxic Religion in Canada," Equal Marriage for Same-Sex Couples, January 18, 2005, www.samesexmarriage.ca/equality/toxic180105.htm

p. 57, "This civil rights movement . . .": Evan Wolfson, *Why Marriage Matters: America, Equality, and Gay People's Right to Marry* (New York: Simon and Schuster, 2004), p. 108.

Chapter 4

p. 59, "Redefining the natural . . . ": Duke Helfand, "Doctrine Disputes Grow As Gays Wed," *Los Angeles Times*, June 19, 2008, http://articles.latimes.com/2008/jun/19/local/me-scripture19

p. 59, "The ancient definition . . . ": Daniela Altimari, "State Supreme Court Legalizes Same-Sex Marriage," *Hartford Courant*, October 11,

2008, www.courant.com/news/connecticut/hc-gaymarriage1011. artoct11,0,1107488.story

p. 59, "The government of a state . . . ": Andrew Sullivan, ed., *Same-Sex Marriage: Pro and Con* (New York: Vintage, 1997), p. 55.

pp. 59, 61, "The legalization of same-sex marriage . . . ": Church of Jesus Christ of Latter-day Saints, "The Divine Institution of Marriage," LDS Newsroom, August 13, 2008, http://newsroom.lds.org/ldsnewsroom/eng/commentary/the-divine-institution-of-marriage

pp. 61–62, "Marriage was founded to propagate . . . ": Roy Rivenburg, "Divided over Gay Marriage," *Los Angeles Times*, March 12, 2004, http://articles.latimes.com/2004/mar/12/entertainment/et-rivenburg12

p. 62, "common sense that . . . ": "Raw Data: Excerpts of Santorum's AP Interview," Fox News, April 22, 2003, www.foxnews.com/story/0,2933,84862,00.html

pp. 62, 64, "That is not correct . . . ": "*Goodridge* v. *Department of Public Health*," Findlaw, November 18, 2003, www.google.com/search?hl=en&source=hp&ie=ISO-8859-1&q=findlaw+goodridge

p. 64, "limiting marriage to . . . ": "*Andersen* v. *King County*," Washington State Supreme Court, July 26, 2006, www.courts.wa.gov/newsinfo/content/pdf/759341opn.pdf, p. 6.

p. 64, "what justification . . . ": "*Lawrence et al.* v. *Texas*," Findlaw, 2003, http://caselaw.lp.findlaw.com/scripts/getcase.pl?court=US&vol=000&invol=02-102

p. 64, "Exceptions do not . . . ": Andrew Sullivan, ed., *Same-Sex Marriage: Pro and Con* (New York: Vintage, 1997), p. 56.

p. 64, "It is true that some . . .": Church of Jesus Christ of Latter-day Saints, "The Divine Institution of Marriage."

p. 65, "A bit of dialogue . . . ": Adam Liptak, "In Battle Over Gay Marriage, Timing May Be Key," *New York Times*, October 27, 2009.

p. 66, "People have a basic . . . "Joseph Ratzinger, "Considerations Regarding Proposals to Give Legal Recognition to Unions between Homosexual Persons," July 2003, www.vatican.va/roman_curia/congregations/cfaith/documents/rc_con_cfaith_doc_20030731_homosexualunions_en.htmlhttp://thebulletin.us/articles/2009/04/17/commentary/op-eds/doc49e7f8bdd01b1083898202.txt

p. 67, "Some scientists, noting . . . ": Louise Gray, "Homosexual Behavior Widespread in Animals according to New Study," Telegraph.co.uk, June

16, 2009, www.telegraph.co.uk/science/science-news/5550488/Homosexual-behaviour-widespread-in-animals-according-to-new-study.html

p. 68, "If it were not for kids . . . ": Roy Rivenburg, "Divided over Gay Marriage," *Los Angeles Times*, March 12, 2004, http://articles.latimes.com/2004/mar/12/entertainment/et-rivenburg12

p. 68, "[T]he vast majority of . . . " American Psychological Association, "Adoption and Co-parenting of Children by Same-Sex Couples," APA Document Reference no. 200214, November 2002, www.google.com/search?hl=en&source=hp&ie=ISO-8859-1&q=american+psychological+association+same-sex+adoption

p. 69, "The Canadian Department . . . ": Paul Hastings et al., "Children's Development of Social Competence across Family Types," Canadian Department of Justice, July 2006, http://74.125.113.132/search?q=cache:WfVbDNI5q1EJ:www.samesexmarriage.ca/docs/Justice_Child_Development.pdf+%22children%27s+development+of+social+competence+across%22&cd=1&hl=en&ct=clnk&gl=us&ie=UTF-8

p. 69, "Children do best when ...": Sarah Wildman, "Children Speak for Same-Sex Marriage," *New York Times*, January 21, 2010.

p. 70, "it is best to. . . ": Evan Wolfson, *Why Marriage Matters: America, Equality, and Gay People's Right to Marry* (New York: Simon and Schuster, 2004), pp. 88–97.

p. 70, "Traditional marriage provides . . . ": Church of Jesus Christ of Latter-day Saints, "The Divine Institution of Marriage."

p. 70, "seed beds from which . . . ": Susan Ferriss, "Prop 8 Witness Says Gay Marriage Undermines Traditional Marriage," *Sacramento Bee*, January 27, 2010, www.mcclatchydc.com/2010/01/27/v-print/83133/prop-8-witness-says-gay-marriage.html

p. 71, "There is no good reason . . . ": Sarah Wildman, "Children Speak for Same-Sex Marriage," *New York Times*, January 21, 2010.

p. 71, "when two adults participate ... ": American Academy of Pediatrics, "Coparent or Second-Parent Adoption by Same-Sex Parents, " *Pediatrics* 109 (February 2002): 339–340 (reaffirmed 1 February 2010), http://aappolicy.aappublications.org/cgi/content/full/pediatrics;109/2/339

p. 71, "It doesn't make . . . ": Sarah Wildman, "Children Speak for Same-Sex Marriage," *New York Times*, January 21, 2010.

p. 71, "Arguing for the passage of ...": "Proposition 8," California General Election Official Voter Information Guide, November 4, 2008, http://

voterguide.sos.ca.gov/past/2008/general/argu-rebut/argu-rebutt8.htm

pp. 71–72, "If the gay marriage ruling . . . ": "Proposition 8," California General Election Official Voter Information Guide, November 4, 2008, http://voterguide.sos.ca.gov/past/2008/general/argu-rebut/argu-rebutt8.htm

p. 72, "Don't be tricked . . . ": "Proposition 8," California General Election Official Voter Information Guide, November 4, 2008, http://voterguide.sos.ca.gov/past/2008/general/argu-rebut/argu-rebutt8.htm

p. 72, "It doesn't bother me . . . ": Sarah Wildman, "Children Speak for Same-Sex Marriage," *New York Times*, January 21, 2010.

p. 72, "It's always the same story . . .": Peter Bronson, "Gay Marriage Is a Topic Wired with Explosives," November 20, 2003, http://www.enquirer.com/editions/2003/11/20/loc_bronson20.html

p. 73, "a homosexual orientation . . . ": Andrew Sullivan, ed., *Same-Sex Marriage: Pro and Con* (New York: Vintage, 1997), p. 67.

p. 74, "need to contain ...": Joseph Ratzinger, "Considerations Regarding Proposals to Give Legal Recognition to Unions between Homosexual Persons," July 2003, www.vatican.va/roman_curia/congregations/cfaith/documents/rc_con_cfaith_doc_20030731_homosexual-unions_en.html

p. 74, "Whatever else it is ...": Ronald Reagan, "Two Ill-Advised California Trends," *Los Angeles Herald-Examiner*, November 1, 1978.

Chapter 5

p. 75, "Homosexual marriage directly attacks . . . ": Eugene Volokh, "Same-Sex Marriage and Slippery Slopes," *Hofstra Law Review*, May 22, 2008: 146–147, www.law.ucla.edu/volokh/#SAMESEX

p. 75, "We must not allow . . . ": Sara Diamond, *Not by Politics Alone: The Enduring Influence of the Christian Right* (New York: Guilford Press, 2000), p. 171.

p. 75, "Without a moral . . . ": Cal Thomas, "Marriage Redefined." Townhall.com, November 18, 2003, townhall.com/columnists/CalThomas/2003/11/18/marriage_redefined

p. 76, "From a conservative standpoint . . . ": Karl Vick, "Same-Sex Marriage Set for Big Day in Federal Court," *Washington Post*, January 11, 2010, www.washingtonpost.com/wp-dyn/content/article/2010/01/10/AR2010011002606.html

p. 76, "It's impossible to be completely …": Susan Ferriss, "Prop 8 Witness Says Gay Marriage Undermines Traditional Marriage," *Sacramento Bee*, January 27, 2010, www.mcclatchydc.com/2010/01/27/v-print/83133/prop-8-witness-says-gay-marriage.html

p. 76, "Almost all the reasons … ": Volokh, p. 143.

p. 77, "The problem I have … ": Daniel Pinello, *America's Struggle for Same-Sex Marriage* (Cambridge, UK: Cambridge University Press, 2006).

p. 78, Hyde: People don't think . . . ": Andrew Sullivan, ed., *Same-Sex Marriage: Pro and Con* (New York: Vintage, 1997), pp. 227–228.

p. 79, "It might be asked … ": Joseph Ratzinger, "Considerations Regarding Proposals to Give Legal Recognition to Unions between Homosexual Persons," July 2003, www.vatican.va/roman_curia/congregations/cfaith/documents/rc_con_cfaith_doc_20030731_homosexual-unions_en.html

p. 79, "it may be true … ": Church of Jesus Christ of Latter-day Saints, "The Divine Institution of Marriage," LDS Newsroom, August 13, 2008, http://newsroom.lds.org/ldsnewsroom/eng/commentary/the-divine-institution-of-marriage

p. 81, "Marriage, while from . . . ": *"Reynolds* v. *United States*, 98 U.S. 145 (1878)," Findlaw, http://caselaw.lp.findlaw.com/cgi-bin/getcase.pl?court=us&vol=98&invol=145

p. 81, "Polygamy has always been . . . ": *"Reynolds* v. *United States*, 98 U.S. 145 (1878)," Findlaw, http://caselaw.lp.findlaw.com/cgi-bin/getcase.pl?court=us&vol=98&invol=145

p. 82, "If the Supreme Court . . . ": Raw Data: Excerpts of Santorum's AP Interview," Fox News, April 22, 2003, www.foxnews.com/story/0,2933,84862,00.html

p. 82, "Polygamy is a choice . . . ": Roy Rivenburg, "Divided over Gay Marriage," *Los Angeles Times*, March 12, 2004, http://articles.latimes.com/2004/mar/12/entertainment/et-rivenburg12.

p. 83, "Slippery-slope diversions . . . ": Evan Wolfson, *Why Marriage Matters: America, Equality, and Gay People's Right to Marry* (New York: Simon and Schuster, 2004), p. 71.

p. 84, "Almighty God . . . ": *"Loving* v. *Virginia*, 388 U.S. 1 (1967)," Findlaw, 1967, http://caselaw.lp.findlaw.com/scripts/getcase.pl?court=US&vol=388&invol=1

p. 86, "Sociologists now estimate . . . ": *Loving* v. *Virginia*, 388 U.S. 1 (1967)."

p. 86, "Imagine the injury to our nation . . . ": Evan Wolfson, *Why Marriage Matters: America, Equality, and Gay People's Right to Marry* (New York: Simon and Schuster, 2004), p. 70.

p. 87, "have not demonstrated . . . ": Michael Mello, *Legalizing Gay Marriage* (Philadelphia: Temple University Press, 2004), pp. 39, 216–223.

pp. 87–88, "Whatever the history ..."; "*Andersen* v. *King County*," Washington Courts, July 26, 2006, p. 26, www.courts.wa.gov/newsinfo/?fa=newsinfo.internetdetail&newsid=707

p. 88, "full-scale retreat". . . "more fully developed . . .": "*Goodridge* v. *Department of Public Health*," Findlaw, November 18, 2003, www.google.com/search?hl=en&source=hp&ie=ISO-8859-1&q=findlaw+goodridge

p. 88, "[T]he historical background . . . " : "*Hernandez* v. *Robles* (2006 NY Slip Op 05239)," New York State Law Reporting Bureau, July 6, 2006, www.courts.state.ny.us/reporter/3dseries/2006/2006_05239.htm

p. 89, "I believe all Americans . . . ": Mildred Loving, "Loving for All," June 12, 2007, http://search.atomz.com/search/?sp_a=sp1003e2ff&sp_q=mildred+loving&sp_p=all&sp_f=ISO-8859-1

p. 89, "Are gay people denied . . . ": Evan Wolfson, *Why Marriage Matters: America, Equality, and Gay People's Right to Marry* (New York: Simon and Schuster, 2004), p. 176.

p. 89, "Gay rights, after all . . . ": Wolfson, *Why Marriage Matters: America, Equality, and Gay People's Right to Marry*, p. 178.

p. 89, "African-American civil rights icons . . . ": Wolfson, *Why Marriage Matters: America, Equality, and Gay People's Right to Marry*, pp. 57–60, 159–182.

pp. 89, 91, "We don't want . . . ": Wolfson, *Why Marriage Matters: America, Equality, and Gay People's Right to Marry*, p. 17.

p. 91, "One opponent ridiculed . . . ": Andrew Sullivan, ed., *Same-Sex Marriage: Pro and Con* (New York: Vintage, 1997), p. 66.

p. 91, "It is not the purpose . . . ": Church of Jesus Christ of Latter-day Saints, "The Divine Institution of Marriage."

p. 91, "are trying to hijack . . . ": Eric Deggans, "Gay Rights and Civil Rights." *St. Petersburg Times*, January 18, 2004, www.sptimes.com/2004/01/18/news_pf/Perspective/Gay_rights__civil_rig.shtml

p. 91, "Yet he supported a . . . ": Deggans, "Gay Rights and Civil Rights."

p. 91, "For them to compare . . . ": Deggans, "Gay Rights and Civil Rights."

p. 91, "As an African American . . . ": Evan Wolfson, *Why Marriage Mat-*

ters: America, Equality, and Gay People's Right to Marry (New York: Simon and Schuster, 2004), p. 165.

p. 91, "If the K.K.K. opposes . . . ": Lynette Clemetson, "Both Sides Court Black Churches in the Battle over Gay Marriage," *New York Times*, March 1, 2004, www.nytimes.com/2004/03/01/us/both-sides-court-black-churches-in-the-battle-over-gay-marriage.html?pagewanted=all

p. 92, "CALIFORNIANS HAVE NEVER . . . ": "Proposition 8," California General Election Official Voter Information Guide, November 4, 2008, http://voterguide.sos.ca.gov/past/2008/general/argu-rebut/argu-rebutt8.htm

p. 92, "[W]hat is at stake . . . ": *Goodridge* v. *Department of Public Health*.

p. 92, "The dissenting judges stated . . . ": J. Clark Kelso, "State Supreme Court Reinforces Basic Freedoms," *California Bar Journal*, September 2008, www.calbar.ca.gov/state/calbar/calbar_cbj.jsp?sCategoryPath=/Home/Attorney%20Resources/California%20Bar%20Journal/September2008&sCatHtmlPath=cbj/2008-09_TH_01_supreme-court.html&sCatHtmlTitle=Top%20Headlines

pp. 92–93, "As a self-governing nation . . . ": Mario Diaz, "What's This I Hear about a Challenge to Marriage in California?" Concerned Women for America, January 13, 2010, www.cwfa.org/articledisplay.asp?id=18265&department=LEGAL&categoryid=family

pp. 93–94, "This came before us . . . ": Michael Mello, *Legalizing Gay Marriage* (Philadelphia: Temple University Press, 2004), p. 256.

p. 94, "[T]he fact is that . . . ": Mario Diaz, "What's This I Hear about a Challenge to Marriage in California?" Concerned Women for America, January 13, 2010.

Chapter 6

pp. 95–96, "The reality is that . . . ": Kate Zernike, "Amid Small Victories, Advocates Lose the Marquee Battles," *New York Times*, December 3, 2009.

p. 96, "The people of the nation . . . ": Nicholas Confessore and Jeremy Peters, "Foe of Gay Marriage Says It's Nothing Personal," *New York Times*, November 10, 2009.

p. 100, "we have the right to . . .": Annie Kelly, "Gay Argentine Couple's Wedding Plans Divide an Entire Continent," *The Observer*, November 29, 2009, http://www.guardian.co.uk/world/2009/nov/29/latin-america-first-gay-wedding

p. 103, "the free uniting of . . . ": "Mexico City Backs Gay Marriage in Latin American First," BBC News, December 21, 2009, http://news. bbc.co.uk/2/hi/8425269.stm

p. 103, "lower than pigs . . .": Associated Press, "Mugabe: No Gay Rights in Zimbabwe," http://abcnews.go.com/International/ wireStory?id=10207764

p. 104, "Homosexuals can forget about . . .": Jeffrey Gettleman, "Ugandan Who Spoke Up for Gays Is Beaten to Death," *New York Times,* January 27, 2011, http://www.nytimes.com/2011/01/28/world/ africa/28uganda.html

p. 104, "civil unions are separate ...": "Report of the Vermont Commission on Family Recognition and Protection," Office of Legislative Council, April 21, 2008. www.leg.state.vt.us/WorkGroups/FamilyCommission/VCFRP_Report.pdf

p. 105, "Although marriage and civil unions . . . ": Daniela Altimari, "State Supreme Court Legalizes Same-Sex Marriage," *Hartford Courant,* October 11, 2008, www.courant.com/news/connecticut/hc-gaymarriage 1011.artoct11,0,1107488.story

p. 107, "to invalidate . . . ": Edwin Meese, "Stacking the Deck against Proposition 8," *New York Times*, January 20, 2010.

p. 107, "I love them . . . ": Nicholas Confessore and Jeremy Peters, "Foe of Gay Marriage Says It's Nothing Personal," *New York Times*, November 10, 2009.

All websites were accurate and accessible as of February 24, 2011.

Further Information

Books

Andryszewski, Tricia. *Same-Sex Marriage*. Minneapolis: Twenty-First Century Books, 2008.

Baird, Robert, and Stuart Rosenbaum, eds. *Same-Sex Marriage: The Moral and Legal Debate*. Amherst, NY: Prometheus Books, 1997.

Friedman, Laurie S. ed. *Gay Marriage: An Opposing Viewpoints Guide*. Detroit: Greenhaven Press, 2008.

Stefoff, Rebecca. *Marriage*. New York: Benchmark Books, 2006.

Sullivan, Andrew, ed. *Same-Sex Marriage: Pro and Con*. New York: Vintage, 1997.

Wardle, Lynn, et al., eds. *Marriage and Same-Sex Unions: A Debate*. Westport, CT: Praeger, 2003.

Websites

Children of Lesbians and Gays Everywhere (COLAGE)
www.colage.org/

Christian Coalition
www.cc.org/

Concerned Women for America (CWA)
www.cwfa.org/about.asp

Egale Canada
www.egale.ca/

Gay and Lesbian Advocates and Defenders (GLAD)
www.glad.org/

Parents, Families, and Friends of Lesbians and Gays (PFLAG)
http://community.pflag.org/Page.aspx?pid=194&srcid=-2

Protect Marriage
www.protectmarriage.com/

All Internet sites were available and accurate as of January 24, 2011.

Bibliography

Articles

"Aguda, O.U. Oppose N.Y. Same-Sex Marriage Bill." *JTA*, May 8, 2009, http://jta.org/news/article/2009/05/08/1005028/agudath-ou-oppose-ny-same-sex-marriage-bill

Altimari, Daniela. "State Supreme Court Legalizes Same-Sex Marriage." *Hartford Courant*, October 11, 2008, www.courant.com/news/connecticut/hc-gaymarriage1011.artoct11,0,1107488.story

Amestoy, Jeffrey. "Uncommon Humanity: Reflections on Judging in a Post-Human Era." *New York University Law Review* 78 (November 2003) 1581–1595, http://www1.law.nyu.edu/journals/lawreview/issues/vol78/no5/index.html

"Anglican Church around the World." BBC News, July 15, 2008, http://news.bbc.co.uk/2/hi/in_depth/3226753.stm

Barr, Bob. "The Federal Marriage Amendment: Why Conservatives and Liberals Alike Should Be Very Glad It Failed." Findlaw, July 16, 2004, http://writ.news.findlaw.com/commentary/20040716_barr.html

Barrionuevo, Alexei. "Argentina Approves Gay Marriage, in a First for Region." *New York Times*, July 16, 2010.

Bhikkhu, Mettanando. "Religion and Same-Sex Marriage." *Bangkok Post*, July 13, 2005, www.buddhistchannel.tv/index.php?id=70,1429,0,0,1,0

Bourassa, Kevin, and Joe Varnell. "Purging Toxic Religion in Canada: Gay Marriage Exposes Faith-Based Bigotry." Equal Marriage for Same-Sex Couples, January 18, 2005, www.samesexmarriage.ca/equality/toxic180105.htm

Carpenter, Dale. "The Federal Marriage Amendment: Unnecessary, Anti-Federalist, and Anti-Democratic." *Policy Analysis*, Cato Institute, June 1, 2006, www.cato.org/pub_display.php?pub_id=6379%22

Chahal, Devinder Singh. "Same-Sex Unions and Sikhism." *Sikh Times*, February 20, 2005, www.sikhtimes.com/news_022005a.html

Chaney, Jen. "'8: The Mormon Proposition': Audacious Look at Church's Role in Gay-Marriage Ban." *Washington Post*, January 30, 2010, www.washingtonpost.com/wp-dyn/content/article/2010/01/29/AR2010012904041.html

Church of Jesus Christ of Latter-day Saints. "California and Same-Sex Marriage." LDS Newsroom, June 30, 2008, http://newsroom.lds.org/ldsnewsroom/eng/commentary/california-and-same-sex-marriage

———. "The Divine Institution of Marriage," LDS Newsroom, August 13, 2008, http://newsroom.lds.org/ldsnewsroom/eng/commentary/the-divine-institution-of-marriage

Clemetson, Lynette. "Both Sides Court Black Churches in the Battle over Gay Marriage." *New York Times*, March 1, 2004, www.nytimes.com/2004/03/01/us/both-sides-court-black-churches-in-the-battle-over-gay-marriage.html?pagewanted=all

Confessore, Nicholas, and Jeremy Peters. "Foe of Gay Marriage Says It's Nothing Personal." *New York Times*, November 10, 2009.

Cooperman, Alan. "Conservative Rabbis Allow Ordained Gays, Same-Sex Unions." *Washington Post*, December 7, 2006, www.washingtonpost.com/wp-dyn/content/article/2006/12/06/AR2006120601247.html

Crumley, Bruce. "France Overruled on Gay Adoption." *Time*, January 24, 2008, www.time.com/time/world/article/0,8599,1706514,00.html

Deggans, Eric. "Gay Rights and Civil Rights." *St. Petersburg Times*, January 18, 2004, www.sptimes.com/2004/01/18/news_pf/Perspective/Gay_rights__civil_rig.shtml

Diaz, Mario. "What's This I Hear about a Challenge to Marriage in California? I Thought the People Had Voted." Concerned Women for America, January 13, 2010, www.cwfa.org/articledisplay.asp?id=18265&department=LEGAL&categoryid=family

Dobner, Jennifer. "Film Focuses on Mormon Role in Gay Marriage Ban." AP, January 23, 2010, http://abcnews.go.com/Entertainment/wireStory?id=9643209

Dolan, Maura. Witnesses in Prop. 8 Trial Examine History of Marriage, Gays." *Los Angeles Times*, January 13, 2010, http://articles.latimes.com/2010/jan/13/local/la-me-prop8-trial13-2010jan13

Duncan, William. "Washington Supreme Court Upholds State's Ban On Gay Marriage." NARTH, July 26, 2006, www.narth.com/docs/states-ban.html

Eleveld, Kerry. "White House Says No to Antigay Referenda," *Advocate*, October 16, 2009, www.advocate.com/News/Daily_News/2009/10/16/White_House_Issues_Statement_on_Maine_Washington/

Falk, Aaron. "Gays Greatest Threat to America, Buttars Says." *Deseret News* (Salt Lake City), February 19, 2009, www.deseretnews.com/article/1,5143,705285940,00.html

Ferriss, Susan. "Prop 8 Witness Says Gay Marriage Undermines Traditional Marriage." *Sacramento Bee*, January 27, 2010, www.wamarriage.org/2010/01/prop-8-witness-says-gay-marriage-undermines-traditional-marriage/

"Gay Marriage Becomes Legal Across Canada." Euronews, July 21, 2005, //prop-www.euronews.net/2005/07/21/gay-marriage-becomes-legal-across-canada/

"Gay 'Marriage' Law Comes into Force in UK." Euronews, May 12, 2005,www.euronews.net/2005/12/05/gay-marriage-law-comes-into-force-in-uk/

Gher, Jaimie. "Polygamy and Same-Sex Marriage—Allies or Adversaries within the Same-Sex Marriage Movement?" *William and Mary Journal on Women and the Law*, 2008, http://works.bepress.com/jaime_gher/1/

Gledhill, Ruth. "Gay Marriage Approval Sounds Death Knell for Anglican Unity." *Times* (London), July 17, 2009, www.timesonline.co.uk/tol/comment/faith/article6716407.ece

Gledhill, Ruth, and Rosemary Bennett. "Anglican Bishops Back End to Ban on Gay Civil Partnerships in Church." *Times* (London), February 23, 2010, www.timesonline.co.uk/tol/comment/faith/article7037062.ece

Goodnough, Abby. "Maine's Vote on Same-Sex Marriage Is Called Close and Crucial." *New York Times*, October 28, 2009.

———. "New Hampshire Legalizes Same-Sex Marriage." *New York Times*, June 3, 2009.

Goodman, Ellen. "Texas Two-step and the Gay Divorce Fandango." *Saratogian*, October 9, 2009.

Grace, Francie. "Conservative Jewish Seminary to Allow Gays." CBS News, March 27, 2007, www.cbsnews.com/stories/2007/03/27/national/main2611436.shtml

Gray, Louise. "Homosexual Behavior Widespread in Animals according to New Study." *Telegraph.co.uk*, June 16, 2009, www.telegraph.co.uk/science/science-news/5550488/Homosexual-behaviour-widespread-in-animals-according-to-new-study.html

Greenberger, Scott. "Bills Aim to Bar Adoption by Gays." Cox News Service, February 13, 1999, www.glapn.org/sodomylaws/usa/texas/txnews28.htm

Grossman. Joanna. "The Fortieth Anniversary of *Loving* v. *Virginia*: The Personal and Cultural Legacy of the Case That Ended Legal Prohibitions on Interracial Marriage, Part 2." Findlaw, June 12, 2007, http://writ. news.findlaw.com/grossman/20070612.html

————. "The Proposed Marriage Protection Act: Why It May Be Unconstitutional." Findlaw, July 27, 2004, http://writ.news.findlaw.com/grossman/20040727.html

————. "The Vermont Legislature, Inventor of the "Civil Union," Grants Full Marriage Rights to Same-Sex Couples. . . ." Findlaw, April 13, 2009, http://writ.news.findlaw.com/grossman/20090413.html

Grynbaum, Michael. "From the Floor and the Heart, Senators Make an Issue Personal." *New York Times*, December 3, 2009.

Haigh, Susan. "Decade-Long Battle to Allow Gay Marriage in Conn. Will End With Governor's Expected Signature." AP, June 20, 2009, www.sfexaminer.com/nation/ap/48687447.html

Hakim, Danny, and Jeremy Peters. "Same-Sex Marriage Faces an Uphill Battle in Albany, If It Makes It to a Vote." *New York Times*, November 9, 2009.

Helfand, Duke. "Doctrine Disputes Grow As Gays Wed." *Los Angeles Times*, June 19, 2008, http://articles.latimes.com/2008/jun/19/local/me-scripture19

Helie, Anissa. "Holy Hatred: Homosexuality in Muslim Countries." Afrol News, www.afrol.com/features/10270

"Iran: Is There an Anti-Homosexual Campaign?" Radio Free Europe, September 1, 2005, www.rferl.org/content/article/1061077.html

Jayson, Sharon. "Divorce Declining, but So Is Marriage." *USA Today*, July 18, 2005, www.usatoday.com/news/nation/2005-07-18-cohabit-divorce_x.htm

Kellie, Annie. "Gay Argentine Couple's Wedding Plans Divide an Entire Continent." *Observer*, November 29, 2009, www.guardian.co.uk/world/2009/nov/29/latin-america-first-gay-wedding

Kelso, J. Clark. "State Supreme Court Reinforces Basic Freedoms." *California Bar Journal*, September 2008, http://archive.calbar.ca.gov/Archive.aspx?articleId=93582&categoryId=93501&month=9&year=2008

Kwon, Lillian. "Anglican Head Reprimands US Church over Lesbian Bishop." *Christian Post*, May 29, 2010, www.christiantoday.com/article/anglican.head.reprimands.us.church.over.lesbian.bishop/25997.htm

"Latin America Sees Its First Same-Sex Marriage." CNN, December 29, 2009, http://edition.cnn.com/2009/WORLD/americas/12/28/argentina.gay.marriage/

"Latin America's First Gay Marriage Halted." CNN, December 1, 2009, www.cnn.com/2009/WORLD/americas/11/30/argentina.gay.marriage/index.html

Lewis, John. "At a Crossroads on Gay Unions." *Boston Globe*, October 25, 2003, www.boston.com/news/globe/editorial_opinion/oped/articles/2003/10/25/at_a_crossroads_on_gay_unions/

Liptak, Adam. "In Battle on Marriage, The Timing May Be the Key." *New York Times*, October 27, 2009.

Loving, Mildred." Loving for All." June 12, 2007, www.freedomtomarry.org/page/-/files/pdfs/mildred_loving-statement.pdf

"Marriage Will Be Defined Nationally—but How: Interview with Wayne Allard." *USA Today*, February 17, 2004, www.usatoday.com/news/opinion/editorials/2004-02-17-marriage_x.htm

McKinley, Jesse. "Backers of Gay Marriage Rethink California Push." *New York Times*, July 27, 2009.

————. "Fight to Reverse California's Same-Sex Marriage Ban Heads to Courtroom." *New York Times*, January 11, 2010.

————. "Proposition 8 Trial Pauses, but Not for Ruling." *New York Times*, January 28, 2010.

Meese, Edwin, III. "Stacking the Deck against Proposition 8." *New York Times*, January 20, 2010.

Melloy, Kilian. "Frank Will Not Support DOMA Repeal." edgeBoston, September 14, 2009, www.edgeboston.com/index.php?ch=news&sc=&sc2=news&sc3=&id=96326

Mujuzi, Jamil. "The Absolute Prohibition of Same-Sex Marriages in Uganda." *International Journal of Law, Policy and the Family*, March 3, 2009, http://lawfam.oxfordjournals.org/cgi/content/abstract/ebp001v1

"New Hampshire Now Fifth State to Allow Same-Sex Marriage." CNN, January 1, 2010, www.cnn.com/2010/POLITICS/01/01/new.hampshire.same.sex/index.html

"Norway Green-lights Gay Marriage," Euronews, June 13, 2008, www.euronews.net/2008/06/13/norway-green-lights-gay-marriage/

Nzeshi, Onwuka. "Nigeria: Homosexuals Kick against Same-Sex Prohibition Bill." Allafrica.com. March 12, 2009, http://allafrica.com/stories/200903120085.html

Peters, Jeremy. "New York Senate Turns Back Bill on Gay Marriage." *New York Times*, December 3, 2009.

"Portugal Passes Gay Marriage Law." Euronews, January 8, 2010, www.euronews.net/2010/01/08/portugal-passes-gay-marriage-law/

Ratzinger, Joseph. "Considerations Regarding Proposals to Give Legal Recognition to Unions between Homosexual Persons." July 2003, www.vatican.va/roman_curia/congregations/cfaith/documents/rc_con_cfaith_doc_20030731_homosexual-unions_en.html

Ravitz, Jessica. "Out-of-Wedlock Births Hit Record High." CNN, April 8, 2009, www.cnn.com/2009/LIVING/wayoflife/04/08/out.of.wedlock.births/index.html#cnnSTCText

"Raw Data: Excerpts of Santorum's AP Interview." Fox News, April 22, 2003, www.foxnews.com/story/0,2933,84862,00.html

Reagan, Ronald. "Editorial: Two Ill-Advised California Trends." *Los Angeles Herald-Examiner*, November 1, 1978.

Regg Cohn, Martin. "Reject Gay Bill, Sikh MPs Told." *Toronto Star*, March 28, 2005, www.equal-marriage.ca/resource.php?id=241

Rivenburg, Roy. "Divided over Gay Marriage." *Los Angeles Times*, March 12, 2004, http://articles.latimes.com/2004/mar/12/entertainment/et-rivenburg12

Safire, William. "On Same-Sex Marriage." *New York Times*, December 1, 2003, www.nytimes.com/2003/12/01/opinion/on-same-sex-marriage.html?pagewanted=1

Shaheen, James. "Gay Marriage: What Would Buddha Do." Huffingtonpost.com, July 13, 2009, www.huffingtonpost.com/james-shaheen/gay-marriage-what-would-b_b_230855.html

Sharon, Susan. "Maine Voters Reject Gay Marriage." NPR, November 4, 2009, www.npr.org/templates/story/story.php?storyId=120080859

Sheeter, Laura. "Latvia Cements Gay Marriage Ban." BBC, December 15, 2005, http://news.bbc.co.uk/2/hi/europe/4531560.stm

"Spanish Gay Marriage Makes History." Euronews, July 12, 2005, www.euronews.net/2005/07/12/spanish-gay-marriage-makes-history/

Sullivan, Gregory. "Same-Sex Marriage: Opening the Door to Polygamy." *Philadelphia Bulletin*, April 17, 2009, http://thebulletin.us/articles/2009/04/17/commentary/op-eds/doc49e7f8bdd01b1083898202.txt

"Swedish Lutherans Allow Gay Marriage." *Euronews*, October 22, 2009, www.euronews.net/2009/10/22/swedish-lutherans-allow-gay-marriage/

Sweet, Laurel. "Landmark Jamaica Plain Gay Couple Calls It Quits." *Boston Herald*, February 3, 2009, www.bostonherald.com/news/regional/view.bg?articleid=1149636&format=text

Syed, Ibrahim. "Same Sex Marriage and Marriage in Islam." Islamic Research Foundation International. www.irfi.org/articles/articles_151_200/same_sex_marriage_and_marriage_i.htm.

Thomas, Cal. "Marriage Redefined." Townhall.com, November 18, 2003, townhall.com/columnists/CalThomas/2003/11/18/marriage_redefined

———. "Raw Judicial Power II." December 27, 1999, www.calthomas.com/index.php?news=215

Tribe, Laurence. "*Lawrence* v. *Texas*: The Fundamental Right That Dare Not Speak Its Name." *Harvard Law Review* 117 (April 2004): 1893–1955.

Tulchin, Allan. "Same-Sex Couples Creating Households in Old Regime France: The Uses of the Affrèrement." *Journal of Modern History* (September 2007): 613–647.

Urbina, Ian. "Nation's Capital Joins 5 States in Legalizing Same-Sex Marriage." *New York Times*, March 4, 2010.

"U.S. Moves to Dismiss First Federal Gay Marriage Case." *USA Today*, June 12, 2009.

Vestal, Christine. "Gay Marriage Decisions Ripe in Calif., Conn." Stateline.org, March 6, 2008, www.stateline.org/live/ViewPage.action?siteNodeId=136&languageId=1&contentId=20695

Vick, Karl. "Same-Sex Marriage Set for Big Day in Federal Court." *Washington Post*, January 11, 2010, www.washingtonpost.com/wp-dyn/content/article/2010/01/10/AR2010011002606.html

Volokh, Eugene. "Same-Sex Marriage and Slippery Slopes." *Hofstra Law Review*, May 22, 2008: 101–147. www.hofstra.edu/PDF/law_lawrev_volokh_vol33no4.pdf.

Wax, Emily. "Namibia Chips Away at African Taboos on Homosexuality." *Washington Post Foreign Service*, October 24, 2005, www.utexas.edu/conferences/africa/ads/1266.html

Wildman, Sarah. "Children Speak for Same-Sex Marriage." *New York Times*, January 21, 2010.

Wilson, Bruce. "Divorce Rate in Gay Marriage-Legal MA Drops to Pre-WWII Level." *Huffingtonpost*, September 3, 2009, www.huffingtonpost.com/bruce-wilson/divorce-rate-in-gay-marri_b_267259.html

Wilson, Robin. "Protect Religious Dissent to Same-Sex Unions." *Albany Times Union*, May 8, 2009.

Yelaja, Prithi. "Sikh Leader's Advice to MPs Dismissed." *Toronto Star*, March 29, 2005, www.equal-marriage.ca/resource.php?id=241

Zernike, Kate. "Amid Small Victories, Advocates Lose the Marquee Battles." *New York Times*, December 3, 2009.

Books

Badgett, Mary. *When Gay People Get Married: What Happens When Societies Legalize Same-Sex Marriage*. New York: New York University Press, 2009.

Baird, Robert, and Stuart Rosenbaum, eds. *Same-Sex Marriage: The Moral and Legal Debate*. Amherst, NY: Prometheus Books, 1997.

Boswell, John. *Christianity, Social Tolerance, and Homosexuality: Gay People in Western Europe from the Beginning of the Christian Era to the Fourteenth Century*. Chicago: University of Chicago Press, 1980.

———. *Same-Sex Unions in Premodern Europe*. New York: Random House, 1994.

Brundage, James. *Law, Sex, and Christian Society in Medieval Europe*. Chicago: University of Chicago Press, 1987.

Crompton, Louis. *Homosexuality and Civilization*. Cambridge, MA: Harvard University Press, 2003.

Diamond, Sara. *Not by Politics Alone: The Enduring Influence of the Christian Right*. New York: Guilford Press, 2000.

English Translation of the Meanings of Al-Qur'an. Houston: Institute of Islamic Knowledge, 1997.

Foucault, Michel. *History of Sexuality. Vol. 1, An Introduction*. Trans. Robert Hurlehy. New York: Vintage, 1990.

Goldberg-Hiller, Jonathan. *The Limits to Union: Same-Sex Marriage and the Politics of Civil Rights*. Ann Arbor: University of Michigan Press, 2002.

Goodich, Michael, ed. *Other Middle Ages: Witnesses at the Margins of Medieval Society*. Philadelphia: University of Pennsylvania Press, 1998.

Halperin, David. *One Hundred Years of Homosexuality and Other Essays on Greek Love*. New York: Routledge, 1990.

Helminiak, Daniel. *What the Bible Really Says about Homosexuality*. New Mexico: Alamo Square Press, 2007 (1994).

Katz, Jonathan. *The Invention of Heterosexuality*. New York, Dutton, 1995.

Kleinbaum, Sharon, and Margaret Wenig. *There's a Place for Us: Gays and Lesbians in the Jewish Community*. Woodstock, VT: Jewish Lights, 2002.

Lochrie, Karma, et al, eds. *Constructing Medieval Sexuality*. Minneapolis: University of Minnesota Press, 1997.

Mello, Michael. *Legalizing Gay Marriage*. Philadelphia: Temple University Press, 2004.

Moore, R. *The Formation of a Persecuting Society: Power and Deviance in Western Europe, 950–1250*. Malden, MA: Blackwell, 1987.

Murray, Jacqueline, ed. *Love, Marriage, and the Family in the Middle Ages*. Orchard Park, NY: Broadview Press, 2001.

New Oxford Annotated Bible. New Revised Standard Version. 3rd ed. Oxford: Oxford University Press, 2007.

Pinello, Daniel. *America's Struggle for Same-Sex Marriage*. Cambridge, UK: Cambridge University Press, 2006.

Rimmerman, Craig, and Clyde Wilcox, eds. *The Politics of Same-Sex Marriage*. Chicago: University of Chicago Press, 2007.

Snyder, R. Claire. *Gay Marriage and Democracy: Equality for All*. Lanham, MD: Rowman and Littlefield, 2006.

Sullivan, Andrew, ed. *Same-Sex Marriage: Pro and Con*. New York: Vintage, 1997.

The Torah: A Modern Commentary. Ed. W. Gunther Plaut. New York: Union of American Hebrew Congregations, 1981.

Vanita, Ruth. *Love's Rite: Same-Sex Marriage in India & the West*. New Delhi: Penguin Books India, 2005.

Wardle, Lynn, et al, eds. *Marriage and Same-Sex Unions: A Debate*. Westport, CT: Praeger, 2003.

Wolfson, Evan. *Why Marriage Matters: America, Equality, and Gay People's Right to Marry*. New York: Simon and Schuster, 2004.

Court Cases and Public Documents

Akinola, Peter. "Message to the Nation." Church of Nigeria, September 14–15, 2006. www.anglican-nig.org/PH2006message2nation.htm

American Academy of Pediatrics. "Coparent or Second-Parent Adoption by Same-Sex Parents." *Pediatrics* 109 (February 2002): 339–340. (reaffirmed 1 February 2010), at http://aappolicy.aappublications.org/cgi/content/full/pediatrics;109/2/339

American Medical Association. "AMA Policy Regarding Sexual Orientation." GLBT Advisory Group. www.ama-assn.org/ama/pub/about-ama/our-people/member-groups-sections/glbt-advisory-committee/ama-policy-regarding-sexual-orientation.shtml

American Psychological Association. "Adoption and Co-parenting of Children by Same-Sex Couples." APA Document Reference no. 200214, November 2002. http://archive.psych.org/edu/other_res/lib_archives/archives/200214.pdf

"*Andersen* v. *King County.*" Supreme Court of the State of Washington, July 26, 2006. www.courts.wa.gov/newsinfo/content/pdf/759341opn.pdf

"*Baehr* v. *Lewin.*" Hawaii Supreme Court, May 5, 1993. www.danpinello.com/Baehr.htm

"Defense of Marriage Act (Public Law 104-199)." September 21, 1996. http://frwebgate.access.gpo.gov/cgi-bin/getdoc.cgi?dbname=104_cong_public_laws&docid=f:publ199.104

"*Finstuen* v. *Crutcher.*" Findlaw, August 3, 2007. http://caselaw.lp.findlaw.com/cgi-bin/getcase.pl?court=10th&navby=docket&no=066213

"*Goodridge* v. *Department of Public Health.*" Findlaw, November 18, 2003. http://fl1.findlaw.com/news.findlaw.com/wp/docs/conlaw/goodridge111803opn.pdf

Hastings, Paul, et al. "Children's Development of Social Competence across Family Types." Canadian Department of Justice, July 2006. http://74.125.113.132/search?q=cache:WfVbDNI5q1EJ:www.samesexmarriage.ca/docs/Justice_Child_Development.pdf+%22children%27s+development+of+social+competence+across%22&cd=1&hl=en&ct=clnk&gl=us&ie=UTF-8

"*Hernandez* v. *Robles* (2006 NY Slip Op 05239)." New York State Law Reporting Bureau, July 6, 2006. www.courts.state.ny.us/reporter/3dseri es/2006/2006_05239.htm

"H.J. Res.88: Proposing an Amendment to the Constitution of the United States Relating to Marriage." June 6, 2006. http://thomas.loc. gov/cgi-bin/query/z?c109:H.J.RES.88

"*In re Marriage Cases* (2008) 43 C4th 757." May 15, 2008. http://online. ceb.com/calcases/C4/43C4t757.htm

Kaminer, Wendy. "Why Is Polygamy Illegal?" Council for Secular Humanism. January 10, 2010. www.secularhumanism.org/index.php?sectio n=library&page=kaminer_28_5

Kennedy, Edward. "Employment Nondiscrimination Act: Text from the Congressional Record." C-SPAN. September 9, 1996. www.c-spanar-chives.org/videoLibrary/clip.php?appid=596956549

"*Lawrence et al.* v. *Texas*." Findlaw, 2003. http://caselaw.lp.findlaw.com/ scripts/getcase.pl?court=US&vol=000&invol=02-102

"*Loving* v. *Virginia*, 388 U.S. 1 (1967)." Findlaw. http://caselaw. lp.findlaw.com/scripts/getcase.pl?court=US&vol=388&invol=1

New Hampshire, State of. "Chapter 59—HB 436-FN-Local—Final Version." March 26, 2009. www.gencourt.state.nh.us/legislation/2009/ HB0436.html

———. "Chapter 61—HB 73—Final Version." June 3, 2009. www. gencourt.state.nh.us/legislation/2009/HB0073.html

Poland—Constitution." October 1997. www.servat.unibe.ch/icl/pl00000 _.html

"Report of the Vermont Commission on Family Recognition and Protection." Office of Legislative Council, April 21, 2008. www.leg.state.vt.us/ WorkGroups/FamilyCommission/VCFRP_Report.pdf

"*Reynolds* v. *U.S.*, 98 U.S. 145 (1878)." Findlaw. http://caselaw.lp.findlaw.com/cgi-bin/getcase.pl?court=us&vol=98&invol=145

Romero, Adam, et al. "Census Snapshot." Williams Institute, December 2007. www.law.ucla.edu/williamsinstitute/publications/USCensusSnapshot.pdf

Southern Baptist Convention. "On Same-Sex Marriage, Resolutions." June 2003. www.sbc.net/resolutions/amResolution.asp?ID=1128

"*Turner* v. *Safley*, 482 U.S. 78 (1987)." Findlaw. http://caselaw.lp.findlaw.com/cgi-bin/getcase.pl?court=US&vol=482&invol=78

United Church of Christ, Resolutions. "Equal Marriage Rights for All." July 4, 2005. www.ucc.org/assets/pdfs/in-support-of-equal-marriage-rights-for-all-with-background.pdf

U.S. General Accounting Office. "Defense of Marriage Act: Update to Prior Report," January 23, 2004. www.gao.gov/products/GAO-04-353R

Van Schaick, Alex. "Bolivia's New Constitution." North American Congress on Latin America, January 21, 2009. https://nacla.org/node/5437

"(*Varnum* v. *Brien*)." Supreme Court of Iowa, April 3, 2009. www.judicial.state.ia.us/Supreme_Court/Recent_Opinions/20090403/07-1499.pdf

Websites

Catholic Answers. "Homosexuality." www.catholic.com/library/Homosexuality.asp

"Proposition 8." California General Election Official Voter Information Guide. http://voterguide.sos.ca.gov/past/2008/general/argu-rebut/argu-rebutt8.htm

All websites were accurate and accessible and as of January 24, 2011.

Index

Page numbers in **boldface** are photographs.

About the Author

JON STERNGASS is a freelance writer specializing in children's nonfiction, who has written more than forty books. Recent works include a book called *Steroids*, in our Controversy! series, and *Terrorism*, in our Debating the Issues series. Born and raised in Brooklyn, Jon Sterngass has a B.A. from Franklin and Marshall College, an M.A. in medieval history from University of Wisconsin—Milwaukee, and a Ph.D. from the City University of New York in nineteenth-century American history. Since 1993, he has lived in Saratoga Springs, New York, with his wife, Karen Weltman, and their sons, Eli and Aaron.